HOW to be CREATIVE

Rediscover your
creativity and live the
life you truly want

Liz Dean

Consultant: Professor Michael Young

CICO BOOKS

LONDON NEW YORK

Published in 2015 by CICO Books
An imprint of Ryland Peters & Small Ltd
20–21 Jockey's Fields   341 E 116th St
London WC1R 4BW   New York, NY 10029

www.rylandpeters.com

10 9 8 7 6 5 4 3 2 1

A CIP catalog record for this book is
available from the Library of Congress
and the British Library.

ISBN: 978 1 78249 167 5

Printed in China
Editor: Rosie Lewis
Designer: Elizabeth Healey
Illustrator: Amy Louise Evans

In-house editor: Dawn Bates
In-house designer: Fahema Khanam
Art director: Sally Powell
Production controller: Sarah Kulasek-Boyd
Publishing manager: Penny Craig
Publisher: Cindy Richards

This book is for my parents,
Eric and Jean.

HOW to be CREATIVE

Contents

introduction 6

CHAPTER ONE
Creative Play 10

CHAPTER TWO
About Time 28

CHAPTER THREE
Creativity as a Path to Empowerment 48

CHAPTER FOUR
Growing Your ideas 68

CHAPTER FIVE
Creative Problem-Solving 82

CHAPTER SiX
Creativity and intuition: Your Creative Sixth Sense 104

CHAPTER SEVEN
Twenty Ways to Be Creative Every Day 122

Words and Phrases and Chapter Notes 140

Bibliography 142

index 143

Acknowledgments 144

introduction

We're all creative. It's what we did naturally as children, with no deadline or purpose other than pleasing ourselves—and what we can still do. Yet, as adults in a competitive marketplace, being "creative" is often perceived as a time-wasting activity that has little bearing on making a success of our lives (unless, of course, we're brilliant, famous, or both). We're told that we must put our toys or crayons aside to do "real" work. Yet recent research shows that those who value their creativity see real benefits in every other aspect of life: we can become more effective and productive in our careers and more communicative in our relationships, and, above all, reconnect with our authentic selves, so that we make life choices that support our well-being. In this book we will learn how to drop self-judgment, find the creative flow, and really please ourselves again.

Creativity is an innate part of who we are, and when we give creativity space, whether deliberately or accidentally, it manifests instantly. We all know someone who took up a new hobby because they were temporarily unable to work or otherwise be active. My close friend Karen realized that she could bake and make mosaics while she was recovering from cancer; another friend, Guy, was made redundant and discovered drawing. This is the power of creativity, to jump into the space our circumstances allow. But it needn't take enforced rest and the threat of boredom to kickstart your creativity; you can be creative at any time, and the benefits are infinite.

All you need is this book, an open mind, and a Creativity Journal dedicated to your creative work. You might use it as a scrapbook, collecting or pasting in materials you find for your projects; as a notebook for ideas; or as a diary in which you share your experiences. As you try some of the exercises in the following chapters, make a note of the date and write down your observations. As your journal fills up, you'll find it offers you a fascinating view of yourself at the time of writing, and a valuable resource to which you can return many times over.

Yet before I get too excited about the prospect of all the ideas that may flow onto the pages of your journal, let's demystify creative work. It's often seen as an enigma we can't decode, to be done only by those with incredible genius. Professor Margaret Boden, a leading academic in the theory of creativity, offers the following three forms of creativity. Her insights, briefly summarized here, go a long way to help us understand more about creativity and originality:

1 The mash-up: Unfamiliar combinations of familiar ideas

We often see an unfamiliar combination of familiar ideas in poetic imagery and art. Boden calls this "combinational creativity." To get the message, we need to understand the author or artist's references. For example, if we read a poem that used Elvis in a timber yard as a metaphor for fallen fame, we would need to know who Elvis was, and what happens in a timber yard— in that it's certainly not glamorous. The unfamiliar/familiar mash-up has to have a point, and not be random for the sake of inventiveness. Barack Obama and the First Lady were recently Photoshopped as King Louis XVI and Michelle Antoinette, with the caption, "Michelle, the peasants are revolting because they have no jobs." She replies, "Yes, they are revolting, but if [they] want jobs they can come over and do my nails and hair." Of course, to get the satire, we have to understand the references.

Creativity is just connecting things. When you ask creative people how they did something, they feel a little guilty because they didn't really do it, they just saw something ... That's because they were able to connect experiences they've had and synthesize new things.
STEVE JOBS

2 Working it: A new idea in an existing style

Boden calls this form "exploratory creativity," and likens it to having a map, then driving onto a smaller road and seeing things you didn't know existed. These places are on the map, but you wouldn't have noticed them if you hadn't taken a diversion. In art, this means creating a new piece of work within an existing style. In craft, an example is making a patchwork quilt. You'll use existing techniques to make it, but might vary the shapes, sizes, and colors, or perhaps be inspired by a new theme, adding unusual detail.

3 New territory: Original thinking

The third form of creativity is thinking differently, in a way that you haven't thought possible before. This might mean changing your existing style and moving into different territory—what Boden calls "transforming the space." It can be difficult to evaluate something that's truly original because there is little to compare it to; of course, that is part of its originality, the fact that it's entirely different. You may have heard of "the bricks," a key Minimalist installation by the artist Carl Andre, exhibited at Tate Britain in London in the 1970s. People thought the Tate had been conned, and could not see any creativity in the work at all. Named *Equivalent VIII*, the sculpture comprised 120 firebricks arranged in a rectangle. As there was little, if anything, to which it could be compared, it provoked curiosity and uproar: gallery assistant Arthur Payne was quoted as saying that the public "can't make head or tail of them. Nothing has attracted as much attention as they have." When you express your creativity, you may find that your work reflects any or all of Boden's forms. Be open to how your ideas might evolve, and also be inspired by the work of others; you don't need to strive to be "truly" original (see pages 120–121). What you do will always be unique to you.

What's in this book?

This book demonstrates how we can all develop creativity and find more fulfillment in all areas of our lives, benefiting communication, approaches to challenges, self-esteem, and even the way we live in our homes and manage our time. Each chapter is an invitation to look at a particular area of potential, from problem-solving through making time for creative play, through developing an idea from scratch. Included are exercises and case studies, and at the back of the book is a list of words and phrases you can use for Oblique Strategies cards (see page 97) or Six-word Stories (see page 126), or indeed in any way you like.

Chapter 1, Creative Play, shines a light on laughter, doodling, and generally pleasing yourself as a path to creativity. Chapter 2, About Time, explores mindfulness, deadlines, creative resistance, and good boredom, and offers techniques and activities for energy and inspiration—no matter what your schedule. To discover your personal vision, dissolve "block" attitudes, and tell your story, turn to Chapter 3, Creativity as a Path to Empowerment. Chapter 4, Growing Your Ideas, gives you the tools to get into a creative mindset and nurture your projects from inception to expression. Learn, too, how to get committed to your creativity and uncover your talents, and how partnership and community can feed the creative flow. Ever wanted to brainstorm alone? Turn to Chapter 5, Creative Problem-Solving, for ideas; learn mind-mapping, or how to take your problem for a walk. This chapter also includes using strategy cards and "tapping" as a way to work through dilemmas and beat that old enemy—procrastination. Chapter 6, Creativity and Intuition: Your Creative Sixth Sense, will help you trust your inner knowing, while Chapter 7, Twenty Ways to Be Creative Every Day, offers at-a-glance ways to make creativity part of your routine.

You might want to flick through the book and choose an exercise at random, letting your intuition guide you, or work through a whole chapter. You might scribble notes in the margins, doodle alongside the illustrations, turn down pages, or add notes of techniques you've tried. Along with your journal, let this book become a record of your adventures in creativity. And as you become more actively creative, you may find that the idea you begin with evolves. Your goal may initially be a memoir, but you develop an interest in making a photo collage; you may want to redesign an interior but end up writing poetry. Creativity opens up many unexpected possibilities, helping us express ourselves more confidently in different forms.

I hope this book encourages you to express your tastes, ideas, and talents.

CHAPTER ONE

Creative Play

One of the most important elements of creativity is play. As children, we all experienced that feeling of **happy absorption**, where time stood still while we melted into the **flow of the game**, armed with openness and curiosity. As adults, **rediscovering our natural sense of play** feeds our creativity. We can learn to recapture a play state of mind to **reengage with the creative self** within.

Creativity
AS THE KEY TO Happiness

When we play, happy emotions are triggered. We want to play again to experience those joyful emotions. (Remember when you played a game as a child and instantly wanted to play it again … and again?) **Play** therefore has **emotional benefits** for us; we're instinctively meant to play. When we are **absorbed in our activity**, without the pressure of goals, comparison, or competition, we receive the reward of happy feelings. And creativity is easier when we're happy, which is why accessing a state of playfulness can be our **springboard into creativity**.

According to neuroscientist and "rat-tickler" Jaak Panksepp of the Play Research Center at Washington State University, it is likely that the play impulse is hard-wired into the emotional networks of our ancient brain structure.

Panksepp's recent research on play with laboratory rats involved measuring their emotional response to play by being tickled, and he terms the high-frequency chirps emitted by the creatures as "rat laughter." Commenting on the importance of changing our attitudes to play, he also explains the result of this shift could be the building of "cultural institutions that support our joyful lower nature, so important for mental heath." When we recognize that play is hard-wired in the brain, we can begin to see playfulness as an intrinsic part of who we are—rather than a guilty pleasure.

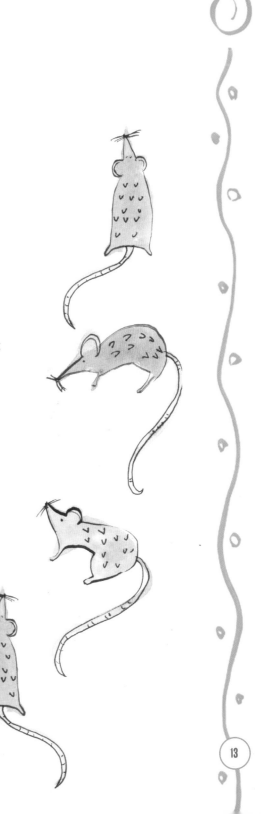

The art of play

Play is the state of mind triggered by an activity, rather than the activity itself. It's usually characterized by some of the following:

- Being fully engaged—in the "flow" (see pages 69–75)
- Having no sense of time
- Not being self-conscious or feeling observed
- Feeling happy, even laughing
- Feeling rewarded
- Feeling that your body knows what it wants to do
- Feeling energized
- Enjoying it regardless of the outcome
- Wanting to do it again

A play attitude can spark creative ideas. Retrieving photos on your computer and playing with the scale because it's entertaining to elongate your nose or to see your cat bright blue might offer an unexpected idea. Making fondant flowers might begin as a half-hour task and go on for hours when you discover that you like doing it, and begin trying different shapes and colors. You may find that dancing or playing music takes you to a different place within yourself, when you're completely captivated by rhythm, as if another part of you comes out to play. Just allow yourself the space to have fun, rather than stepping in to judge your activity: when you play, you're doing what your brain designed you to do to help you experience happiness and contentment.

Creativity is easier when you feel positive

Play helps to generate positive feelings, and it's easier to be creative when you feel positive. It's interesting to note that research shows that those who suffer from anxiety and depression tend to find it more difficult to be creative than those with a more positive outlook. The irony is that being creative can help to generate happiness—but if you're anxious you may find it more difficult to get started. Stress and being overwhelmed can also block the creative pathway, which is why beginning with play can gently open us up to positive emotions and cultivate creativity. Here are some suggestions:

- Move to music or do a doodle (see page 20)
- Recall one happy memory and replay it in your mind
- Cultivate gratitude for three or more things you've received or experienced today (food, warmth, conversation, a working internet connection …). Write them down
- Bring to mind a person and/or a pet you adore
- Laugh

Laughter AS A Creative Tool

Whether we laugh at a joke or find our own laughter within, laughter supports our creative practice and benefits both mind and body.

We know that laughter, like exercise, releases endorphins, the happiness chemical. It also increases blood flow, which helps to protect the heart. It's also a brilliant de-stressor and immunity booster: research by Dr. Lee S. Berk of Loma Linda University, California, and Dr. Stanley Tan, also of Loma Linda University, has suggested that laughter decreases the levels of stress hormones cortisol and adrenalin, and also supports the function of the immune system by increasing the number of immune cells and antibodies.

Laughter is a whole-body experience: we're using our lungs, jaw, mouth, tongue, and all the rest of our body in a physical response. We can throw back our heads or shake with laughter. We don't engage our brain first to decide if something is funny; the body tells us it is. Like creativity itself,

laughter is instinctive, and benefits us wholeheartedly.

Laughter is an expression of our creativity. By seeing the funny side of a situation, we make a new connection in an instant; by laughing, we "get" it—"it" being a new perspective, reality altered by the filter of humor. Comedians offer their own creative take on the everyday, and often put together bizarre combinations of characters, recollections, and events to create comedy. Laughter is our way of showing that they've succeeded in creating something new for us, and often we revere our favorite comedians as national treasures, as we do our athletes.

Creativity often needs the magic seeds of play and laughter. Researcher Avner Ziv found that a group of adolescents who listened to

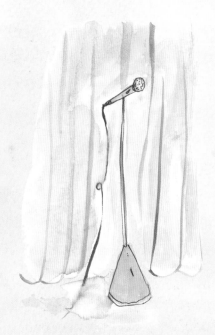

a humorous record performed significantly better in a creativity test than control groups. Roger von Oech, author of the creativity classic *A Whack on the Side of the Head*, says: "There's a close relationship between the 'ha ha' of humor and the 'A-ha!' of discovery. If you can laugh at a problem or situation, perhaps you'll overturn a few assumptions and come up with some fresh ideas."

One way we can access laughter and our personal creativity is through a practice known as Laughter Yoga. Laughter Yoga educator and writer Joe Hoare makes a key distinction between laughter and humor, which explains the unique approach of Laughter Yoga. "Humor is different from laughter. With Laughter Yoga, we don't need jokes—we learn to laugh from the inside, rather than in response to a joke or funny situation. In the West, we think of laughter as something coming from outside ourselves, but in the East and elsewhere, laughter is used as a meditation practice."

Joe finds there is a vital connection between laughter and creativity. He says, "Laughter Yoga is confidence-building —when you laugh, you follow your own direct experience, tapping into your natural creativity. By getting out of our heads and into our bodies through laughter practice, we become able react to what's really happening in the moment."

Through his extensive experience as a group facilitator, Joe explains how the practice "fires up their [students'] zest for life in unexpected ways. And students return to laughter yoga groups because the enjoyment feeds into the rest of their lives. Through laughter, they become aware of just how creative they are.'

Overleaf are Joe's techniques for laughter practice on your own (see also page 140 for more information on his work).

Exercise: Getting ready to laugh

Guidelines

It's best to wear loose clothing, so that you're comfortable and your body can move easily.

While, of course, you can laugh any time, a great time to practice is first thing in the morning, as it helps set a positive tone for the day ahead. You might also laugh at the end of the day, as it helps give perspective on the day's events—you can laugh away worries and anxieties that may have built up.

Start with just a few minutes, then build up to five or ten minutes? Time yourself too?

Warm-up exercises

Before you start laughter exercises, you can do some warm-up exercises. Rather than try to laugh straight away, start by making sounds with your voice to get comfortable with vocalizing sounds. Play with vowel sounds, then add an "H", ie turn them into a laugh —such as He, Ha, Ho, Hu Hi.

Exercise: Fake it until you make it

Research has shown that the body cannot differentiate between real and make-believe emotions (think of the tension you feel when watching an action movie, for example). So when you begin faking an emotion through your physical body, your emotions and mind catch up so it feels genuine and real.

1. Start by making laughter sounds, as in the warm-up.

2. Continue—you might feel some kind of shift happening as you do this and being to laugh. Do it with willingness—in time your fake laugh becomes the real thing. With practice, it becomes an instant warm, genuine, connecting laugh.

3. Try it for five or ten minutes—whatever you feel is right. Observe how Laughter Yoga alters your mood after the practice has ended.

THE Rebel Doodle

The appeal of the doodle is that it's **fun**. Commonly, we doodle when we're not supposed to—during **business meetings**, while on long **phone calls**—and of course we all doodled in the margins of our **school books** during lessons.

Doodling is an expression of the unconscious mind that happens when our focus should be on another task; it's as if the creative part of us wants to have fun, to rebel, while we're supposed to be at our most adult and serious (which is why we may doodle more in formal, organized meetings). Originally meaning "fool," possibly from the German *Dudeltopf* (literally "nightcap," but used in the sense of "simpleton"), the word can be seen positively as meaning "to fool around"—to give our playful side free rein.

The doodler

Artist Gwyneth Leech, who lives in New York City, doodled to pass the time in meetings. She says: "Sitting still and listening at meetings, my hands needed to move constantly and—without my really being aware of it—my paper coffee cups were covered with drawings. These drawings intrigued me, and I followed the thread. The cup form is the same each time, so I gave myself complete permission to draw anything I liked."

Her themes range from cityscapes through local street scenes including New York cabs, to daffodils and sunflowers. She records the date, location, and occasion on the bottom of each cup. Leech has now created over 1,000 painted cups, and her work has been exhibited in the United States, including in the window of the Anthropologie store in Cambridge, Massachusetts, and in London and Edinburgh. The humble doodle has been the recourse of the famous (poet Allen Ginsberg, writer Henry Miller, and President Ronald Reagan, among others), and comprises images sometimes accompanied by words and/or numbers, often with an irreverent tone.

The writer Kurt Vonnegut's word doodle, an illustration in his memoir *A Man Without a Country* (2005), states: "We are here on earth to fart around. Don't let anyone tell you any different."

The fun element of the doodle is part of Google's branding, to celebrate holidays and anniversaries. It was born when the Google founders doodled around the Google logo and put in a stick man to show they were at the Burning Man festival in Nevada. According to Google, "the revised logo was intended as a comical message to Google users that the founders were 'out of office.'" Google has since created around 2,000 Google doodles (and it invites doodle proposals, too—send your Google doodle to proposals@google.com).

Exercise: Do the doodle

1 Have a doodle in your Creativity Journal (see page 6). In time-honored fashion, doodle when you're supposed to be doing something else (take your journal into your next work meeting, have it by you when you're on the phone, or keep it on your lap while you're watching a movie).

2 Review your doodles after a few days. What did you doodle? Common motifs are flowers, arrows, cubes, faces, patterns, and landscapes, but you may have doodled something else (doodle it again here or in the margin while you're reading this).

3 Choose one doodle and make it the basis for a project, or use it as an insight into a way you might approach a piece of work. For example, faces may suggest that there are people you need to collaborate with (see page 80); arrows might point to a clear sense of direction, a need to emphasize an aspect of your work or, literally, an idea for an illustration project. While these interpretations may or may not hit the mark with you, the purpose of the exercise is to explore the meanings of your own doodles and appreciate that all your output, even a doodle, has creative potential.

Why doodling works

Doodle play lets your unconscious mind out of the box without any pressure to create a masterpiece—it's just a doodle, right? The doodle cleverly circumvents the biggest blocks to creativity—judgment and fear of comparison—because it's not categorized as "serious" work. But your doodles still reflect you and your internal processes, helping you to cultivate new approaches and ideas.

Graphic recording: The doodle off the page

Doodling has more recently evolved into a process known as graphic recording. New York artists Image Think work with businesses including NASA, Time Warner, and Johnson & Johnson to record important meetings and conferences in pictures and words in real time, so that audiences can see the artwork being created live, as the meeting happens. According to Image Think, "audiences sense instantly that something different and fun is about to happen that's worth paying attention to." Like Gwyneth Leech's decorated coffee cups, Image Think took doodling off the page and created an art form with structure, purpose—and fun.

What could you do with a doodle?

THE PRINCIPLE OF CREATIVE PLAY:
Do What you Love

All too often, we get hooked on the outcome of a project rather than the process of creating it. While it's almost irresistible to **dream of success** and acknowledgment, this means staking a project on other people's approval, rather than **creating for the sake of it**. This bypasses the learning experience a project can offer us personally, and ties up its potential success with things or people outside our control. Success should be measured by our **enjoyment** of our personal creativity and playfulness.

Many entrepreneurs encounter negativity and even ridicule when they first begin. If they allowed these reactions to affect them, they might even stop their creative work altogether—but a common trait in many of these individuals is that they decide that, even if no one likes what they do, they'll do it anyway, simply because they enjoy it. They honor their projects and put their need to be creative above other people's opinions (or their assumptions about how their work might be received). I'm not saying that anyone should ignore constructive feedback, but do keep the focus on entertaining yourself. That way, your work will hold your passion. Passion is energy, and energy is also currency—money—which often flows from work that is passionate and authentic. Money is a fortunate by-product of creativity, and has nothing to do initially with the creative project itself. See Mary K.'s stories on page 26.

Exercise: **Please yourself**

You can use this exercise daily as a creative warm-up, helping you to get into a playful mindset before you begin your projects.

Ben & Jerry's ice cream stems from childhood friends Ben Cohen and Jerry Greenfield, who worked as students in an ice-cream van, learned to make ice cream on a farm, and liked it. Cohen couldn't taste much and he doesn't have a sense of smell, so when they decided to make their own ice cream, he made up flavors he could taste—just for him.

(1) Make up some ice-cream flavors. Put as many tastes together as you like (hedgehog and brandy?), then go more esoteric—seashore and honey; you get the picture. Now visualize how certain colors, objects, or even experiences might taste: a wedding, disappointment, white linen. Keep inventing.

(2) What else would you do if you had only to please yourself?

Mary K.'s stories

While working part-time in a community library, Mary K. began writing a novel. It took her almost four years, with about seven redrafts, and there were also times when she just put it in a drawer for a while. When she was finally happy with it, a friend suggested that she send it to an agent. Mary was ambivalent about this; while she wanted to share the book, the thought of the agent was daunting. But on meeting Frank, who sold novels to all the big publishers, she became excited and thought she'd let him represent her.

Months and months ticked by, followed by rejection after rejection. After feedback from publishers, her agent gave her the following critique: "The problem is, Mary, that the publishers don't know how to categorize it. It's not chick lit, but it's not what they'd call literary, either—it's between the two." There was little comment on the story, the ideas, or her style—just the fact that no one knew what to do with the book, or how to market it.

Then came a phone call from Frank: "One of the editors wants to meet with you to talk further about the book." Mary was delighted, and she put the phone down feeling a mixture of fear and excitement. Would they want her on their list? Had she finally done it? The meeting came around. "I really like the period of history you've set your novel in," the editor began, all big desk and teeth, "but what I'm really looking at here is a different novel from you, still set in the war years, because I know that stories about servicemen will be big next year because of the war centenary coming up. Could you write me three chapters with these characters?"

"Admittedly, I was nervous about doing this," Mary said afterward to me. "But I saw it as my big chance to impress them, and maybe if I wrote the novel they wanted first, and it was successful, they'd consider my existing work. So I did it—and I've regretted it ever since."

The publisher rejected Mary's new chapters and they never met again.

"It felt like a real setback," she confided. For a time, she couldn't write and felt she'd wasted all her efforts. A month or two later, she and her partner were watching a movie about Woodstock, and Mary thought that might be the basis for another book. So she decided to begin her second novel anyhow, and set it in the 1960s. When she began writing again, it felt different, somehow more free, and she recognized that last time she'd invested too much emotionally in getting published, and having a level of success by which other people would acknowledge her. Now she didn't have to think about anyone but herself.

Of course, this type of story is supposed to end with the line, "and then she was finally discovered by another publisher and is now a million-copy-selling author." This hasn't happened yet; it may happen, or it may not—who knows. Mary is immensely proud of the five novels she has written, all on themes that fascinate her:

"I feel I've been able to express myself through my writing. I now just listen to my inner voice, and concentrate on bringing my characters to life. I follow my own rules. I'd love to be published one day, but this goal has nothing to do with how or why I write."

Mary's story illustrates that commercial writing, with the editor she met, wasn't right for her; and that fixating on a publishing deal led to heartache. It doesn't mean the editor was wrong—she has a business to run, after all, and she knows what sells. But the experience threatened to derail Mary's creativity—until she recognized her real reasons for writing, and how she needed to refocus on herself and her personal motivation rather than change to please a publisher.

CHAPTER TWO

About Time

Not having enough time is one of the greatest **blocks to creativity,** yet it's often self-imposed. When you trust in the creative process and learn to **value your time,** you'll find you begin to take a more **creative attitude** toward primary work and everyday tasks; your whole life approach begins to shift.

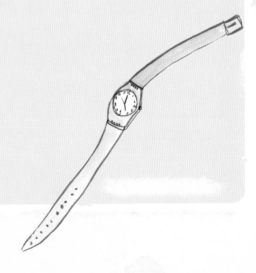

Creativity IS A Priority

Many people claim that they don't have time to be creative. But **creativity is a necessity**, not a luxury or an indulgence; it is essential for our well-being (see page 12). We build exercise into our schedules because it's important for good health, but if we don't make real time for creativity, we're denying ourselves the expression of a fundamental aspect of what it means to be human. We have a **natural need** to create—all of us.

We may sense a small, familiar voice, urging us to do our creative work during a never-ending, hectic week; we might resist its call (see page 36) or try to placate it, and make a bargain: we'll get down to that project when everything else is done. In reality, this means we finally get to our special project when we're tired, yet still sit there, waiting for the inspiration magically to manifest itself. Or, when that creative time comes around, we end up not being creative at all. Instead of making the video, taking photographs, creating a collage or greetings card, working on a poem, reading, singing,

or drawing, we decide we're a bit tired for all that and tune out: channel-hop, check our phones, browse the net, or snack.

Creative projects, however, give us energy, while tune-outs deplete it. Make a list of activities that give you a buzz. You'll find it's the activities that nurture your creativity, rather than tune-outs, which leave you feeling flat and guilty. And good pursuits don't have to be what we'd traditionally define as "artistic"; whatever you love doing is creative work.

Managing time and energy

My friend Liz is a single parent with two teenage children and little family support nearby. Money has always been tight. Liz works full-time in social work and is studying for a diploma, too, but she told me recently that she had taken on an extra job, working eight evenings a month giving complementary therapies to vulnerable people. I was concerned for her—I know she's always exhausted at the end of the week. But Liz was adamant.

"The thing is," she explained, "doing out-of-hours work with the homeless was my calling before I had the kids; when I first went into social work, I worked shifts in a hostel for young people with mental-health problems. I absolutely loved it. Although this new job means working more hours in the week, it doesn't even feel like work. It helps to pay the bills, but I get something back, too."

Liz could have chosen to increase her hours in her day job to earn more money, but she recognized that to manage her energy levels and her time, she needed to do something that inspired her. "I realize that what I'm good at is working with very vulnerable people, and I can make a difference that way," she smiles. "And I've also found that my day job feels a bit more manageable, as though I've got back part of my old self—I'm remembering why I became a social worker."

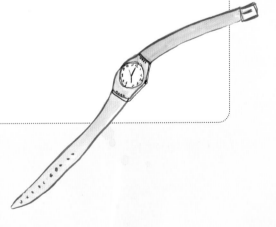

Making Time
FOR YOUR Creativity

- Make a commitment to your creativity by scheduling a weekly date to create. Author and screenwriter Julia Cameron, in her best-seller *The Artist's Way* (1992), calls this the "artist date." Put your creative slot in your phone calendar or diary at the beginning of each week.

- If you're finding it impossible to schedule time for yourself, try the infographic task (see page 34), or begin with the little daily rituals (see page 33). Avoiding making time for creativity can also be a form of resistance (see page 37 for tips on working through this).

- Protect your creative time. Other than for emergencies, make this time sacred. This means choosing your creativity over other daily demands: the pressure to go out, meet with friends, or do the laundry.

- If you find it difficult to shift from work/overthinking mode, try the creative crunch practice (page 74). Another good technique is to write down your mental clutter—scribble a list of what's on your mind, trust that you'll deal with it when you have to (and not now), then put it aside. This helps you to stop rehearsing future tasks and focus on the present to get the most out of the creative slot you've allocated for yourself. (One of your creative slots might be mindfulness practice, which can give the sensation of time actually expanding—see the mindfulness practices on page 42.)

Little daily rituals

- Get up ten minutes earlier each day for six days—that's one hour in total. Spend that time making a list of ideas, or setting a general intention for how you'd like your day to turn out: setting a goal, or just being calm, or having courage if there's a challenge you'll need to deal with, for example. If you're a morning person, getting up early to spend time on your project might work for you—the poet Sylvia Plath would get up before dawn to write while her young children were still asleep.

- If you work during the day, vow to leave your desk for 20 minutes at lunchtime and walk around the outside of the office, go to the park, go see a building close by, or browse in a store; changing your environment can help you to get the most out of the time you have, particularly if you treat yourself to a brief visit to a new place. New experiences help us to cultivate an attitude of openness, which feeds creativity.

Exercise: Make an infographic

Make copies of the blank clock dial, right, and use one for AM and one for PM. Fill the dials in at the end of each day, estimating how much time you've spent on the areas listed. Use a different color for each type of activity. For example, green for sleep, pink for exercise. It might look something like this:

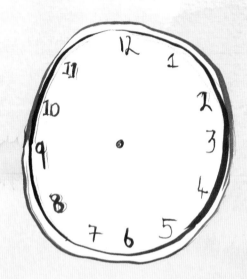

AM routine

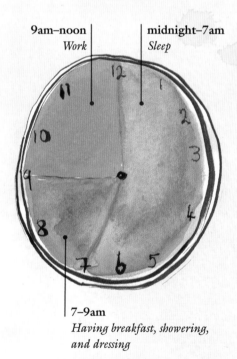

9am–noon
Work

midnight–7am
Sleep

7–9am
Having breakfast, showering, and dressing

PM routine

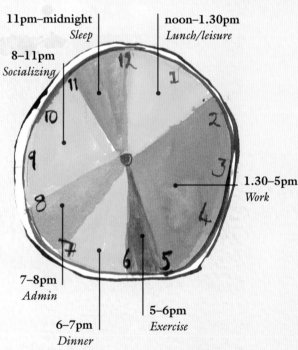

11pm–midnight
Sleep

8–11pm
Socializing

noon–1.30pm
Lunch/leisure

1.30–5pm
Work

5–6pm
Exercise

7–8pm
Admin

6–7pm
Dinner

For the next three days, color in your infographic at the start of each day, apportioning your ideal time spent on the various activities. It's likely that you'll see a positive difference between the first three clocks and the next three when you begin the day with an awareness of time, rather than wondering how it ran away from you. Did you make time for the creative activities you wanted to do?

BENJAMIN FRANKLIN'S DAILY ROUTINE

Benjamin Franklin started his day with the question: 'What good shall I do this day?"
and ended it with the question: "What good have I done today?" The clocks below
show how his day was broken up into different activities.

AM routine

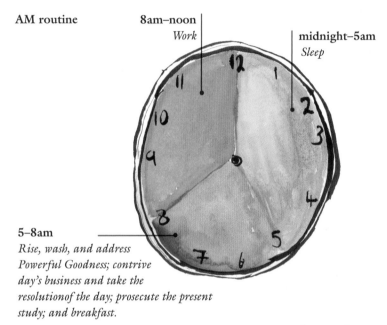

8am–noon
Work

midnight–5am
Sleep

5–8am
*Rise, wash, and address
Powerful Goodness; contrive
day's business and take the
resolutionof the day; prosecute the present
study; and breakfast.*

PM routine

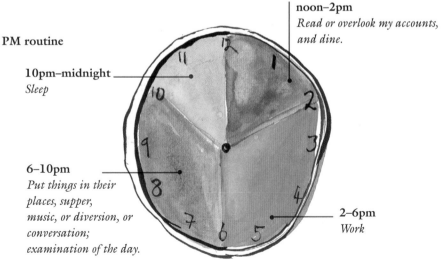

noon–2pm
*Read or overlook my accounts,
and dine.*

10pm–midnight
Sleep

6–10pm
*Put things in their
places, supper,
music, or diversion, or
conversation;
examination of the day.*

2–6pm
Work

Time AND Resistance

So, you've scheduled your creative time. Are you stepping into it **effortlessly**, or are you resisting? You've planned a walk, a trip, or a session writing or making something. You're about to begin, feel edgy, and decide to browse the net for a while first— or anything that will delay you getting going. Your resistance will invent a host of merry excuses: Mercury, the planet of communication, is retrograde; **maybe you shouldn't begin when it's raining,** since that always brings on a low mood; or the contents of the refrigerator are more interesting.

In his best-seller *The War of Art* (2002), the writer Steven Pressfield personifies this feeling of semi-dread before creative time as Resistance (with a capital R). Pressfield sees Resistance as the enemy of the artist. He says: "We experience it as an energy field radiating from a work-in-potential. It's a repelling force … Its aim is to shove us away, distract us, prevent us from doing our work."

In my experience, when you are in a state of resistance, it's because something is at stake. Creativity involves personal risk—you

are allowing part of you, your beliefs and ideas, to take form, and your creative work has the power to change and transform you in a profound way. Resistance likes things to stay as they are. We can see it winning in those who dream and talk about what they want to do, but back off the instant there's a chance to make it happen in the real world. Living with the dream rather than getting down to the work of creating means there's no chance of failure (or success). In this sense, feeling resistance is a sure sign that what you want to create is important. Learn to recognize resistance when it's around, and you'll push through it—and continue with what you set out to do.

Resistance-busting tips

- The aim is to begin. If you can't get going within the first half-hour of creative work, go do something else for an hour, then go back to it. Read, clean, phone, walk … then go back to your creative work. It doesn't matter if you can't keep going for the whole time you've allocated—an hour's productive work is fine.
- Habit helps. The more you keep to your creative timeslot, the easier it becomes.
- Don't judge what you're doing. Reviewing what you did last time gets you into judgment mode, so when you begin, go straight to the next chapter, or the next piece you're making.
- Get into the right-brain mode with the creative crunch exercise on page 74.

Dealing with deadlines

Realistic deadlines can be brilliant motivators, helping you to plan your time and deliver your work. They also help you to break down a project into bite-size, manageable chunks; the author Stephen King writes ten pages (about 2,000 words) every day, seven days a week. He has done this for many years, and is an experienced "deadliner"—he knows what works for him. Dickens's first novel, *The Pickwick Papers*, began in 1836 as a series of sketches originally entitled *The Posthumous Papers of the Pickwick Club*, published every month in the *Morning Chronicle* newspaper. Many a contemporary writer has followed the same path: *Bridget Jones's Diary* (1996) by Helen Fielding began life in *The Telegraph*, while Armistead Maupin's acclaimed novel series *Tales of the City* (1978–), on life in San Francisco in the 1970s and 1980s, appeared in the *San Francisco Chronicle*.

No doubt the strict deadlines motivated the authors—as did the promise of regular paychecks.

From regular deadlines, good habits form. And deadlines can become easier to meet when we've done it all before, when we know, more or less, what will be involved (although this doesn't discount the effort involved in the creating).

Leo's table

Beginning a new project, however, involves more learning, and it may take longer than anticipated to meet a deadline when we really don't know what is involved, or how long it might take. Leo, an administrative manager from Oregon, explains:

"I decided to make a table to mark a family anniversary. It was the first time I'd tried this kind of piece—it was quite ornate, but I wanted to create something really special. The table legs were decorative and involved wood-turning, but I decided to have a go. I'm a planner at heart, and I'd written out a schedule for myself—but I couldn't believe how inaccurate my timing was. It took three weeks to work the first leg, and I thought, "At this rate, it will never be finished on time." I'd already told family members what I was doing, so I couldn't turn around and say that it wouldn't be ready.

"The only thing I could do was to keep on going. By the fourth week, I realized I was starting to speed up. I had learned a skill and now I could repeat it, and by the time I made the fourth leg, I guess that only took me four days. I also stopped thinking about the project as a whole—I just focused on doing one leg at a time. In the end, I felt really satisfied when I not only had finished the table, but I'd mastered a new skill. It gave me the confidence to push myself further."

However we regard deadlines, they always offer a learning experience; we can observe how we react to the deadline and hopefully discover new skills or needs in the process.

Carolyn's bakes

Even professionals, whose reputations depend on delivering on time, come up against occasional deadlines that threaten to derail their creativity.

Carolyn, a wedding baker, took on a huge event with a terrifying deadline: "I had to bake 850 cupcakes in two days—but for some reason, I honestly thought I could do it. I'd done 500 before, and the fee was attractive, so I said yes. But one of the ovens broke down, a kitchen assistant got sick, and I felt completely overwhelmed. For about an hour I couldn't think straight; I was standing in a hot kitchen with 600 bakes done, 250 to go, shaking—I even felt sick with nerves at the thought of letting down the bride on her big day.

"I walked outside and took a deep breath. All I could hold on to was the knowledge that the panic would end, and the sense of sheer relief I'd feel when it was all over this time tomorrow."

Carolyn pleaded with her sister to come over and help, and her sister brought a friend—and eventually the order was delivered on time.

"I promised myself never, ever, to agree to a job like that again—not until I had bigger premises and reserve staff. I guess I learned something about myself that day—that I'd put myself under too much pressure, without thinking of the consequences. I was in danger of hating the business I was in, when in reality baking was, and thankfully still is, my dream job."

Some deadline pressure can make us thrive, and the adrenaline that is released when we're single-minded and focused on one goal gives us a high; sometimes we're pushed out of our comfort zones and even, like Leo, learn a skill relatively quickly because the deadline exists.

Carolyn's experience shows that even professional deadliners can underestimate the time they need, but even the most stressful deadline situation tells you more about the kind of person you are, and how much or how little pressure you need to be motivated.

Setting the right deadlines

Decide what kind of deadliner you are. Do you need lots of last-minute pressure to get finished, or smaller, weekly deadlines?

- Be realistic. It's easy to be overly enthusiastic about what you can deliver, particularly if you have been approached by another person or company to offer a product or service. Avoid agreeing to the deadline until you've had time to consider it. People who value your work will respect your taking appropriate time to come to a decision, and see it as a mark of professionalism.
- Build in time for a learning curve if you will be doing something in a different way from usual, or for the first time
- Build in time for breaks.
- Assume that you'll have unexpected tasks—a short trip away, time to recover from a headache, for example—and times when you need to be positively bored to fuel your ideas (see page 44).

- Build in time for self-care: time to go for walks or to the gym, to be with people you like and who support your project.
- Whatever deadline you decide to go for, add on a day/a week/a month (depending on the length of the job) for good measure.
- When you've set your personal deadline, or agreed to someone else's, check in with yourself. How are you feeling? Notice exactly what's going on in your body. If you feel any tension (other than a vague excitement), the deadline may be too tight. Your body will respond to the deadline for you, and tell you, through physical sensation, what is wrong or right. You might decide, if you are in control of the deadline, that you don't need or want a deadline after all. You'd prefer to go with the flow, and see where your ideas lead.

Mindful Ways
TO MAKE THE MOST
OF Your Time

Mindfulness techniques are a great way to find peace, **reconnect with ourselves**, and make space for our creativity to thrive. May people who practice mindfulness find that it can create a sense of time **slowing down** as they focus on the moment, the here and now.

According to Professor Mark Williams, a mindfulness researcher at Oxford University, "mindfulness cultivates our ability to do things knowing that we're doing them." Dr. Kristin Neff, associate professor in human development at the University of Texas in Austin, describes it as "seeing things exactly as they are, no more, no less." In therapeutic practice, mindfulness combines ancient meditation techniques with cognitive behavioral therapy to treat conditions such as anxiety and depression. In our busy lives, using mindfulness techniques every day can help us to slow down, de-stress, and appreciate each moment as it arrives.

Think about the first time you drove or walked to a new place of work. You probably absorbed everything around you—the sound of the traffic, a tree just in leaf on the left-hand side of the road, the kind of people walking nearby (office workers, children going to school, a strange guy with a clipboard …). It may have felt like a long way. Yet after weeks, months, or years of doing the same route, we can arrive at work barely remembering how we got there. Each morning, the journey has passed in a flash, as if time speeds up whenever we make that same trip.

Practicing daily mindfulness offers a sense of time expanding, because it invites us to experience ourselves wherever we are, slowly and without judgment. When we slow down, we really notice what's happening, and in this noticing our senses become sharper and our imagination comes in to play. It can feel as though we're doing something old, but experiencing it in a new way, with fresh awareness, curiosity, and even wonder: we can really experience being in the moment. Try these mindfulness rituals to see for yourself:

- Take a new route to work
- Contemplate an object
- Meditate for five minutes
- Eat mindfully, without the computer or television in front of you. Before you eat, look at the colors on your plate. Take a small bite, and feel its texture on your tongue. Chew slowly and savor every mouthful. You may find yourself thinking about where the food on your plate has come from. You might begin to feel grateful to the earth for giving you your food. Maybe you recall a feeling triggered by a taste. Is it sour or sweet? What other things in life have felt this sweet?

Exercise: The mindful walk

Walking is something we do every day, often without awareness. Walking with the intention of being mindful of your thoughts, sensations, and the environment can help you to feel calmer and reconnect with your creative self as you pay attention to where you are. Leading mindfulness educator Dr. Patrizia Collard, author of *Journey into Mindfulness* (2013), invited me to join her mindful meditation students for a stroll around the park at the top of her yard.

We began with a short mediation in Patrizia's family room before setting out from the back of the house and heading into the park. Walking without a watch or a cell phone, 15 minutes felt like an hour—in fact, after five minutes I decided time was probably up. I studied the bark on a tree, touched it, and felt its graininess. I began to remember nature walks we'd had as children, touching snowdrops in the park, when we were smaller and closer to the earth. In all, I realized I was beginning to feel calmer, and more interested in little details on the walk—the intricate ironwork on a bench, the faint chirrup of a bird—as if my sight and hearing were becoming more acute. On returning to Patrizia's house, I felt I had experienced a kind of time expansion, a quiet zone in which nothing had felt rushed or urgent.

Try this:
- Decide where you'd like to walk. Set the intention that your walking will be mindful, and leave your cell phone at home.
- Begin to walk by really sensing your feet on the ground as you plant them with each step. Generate the feeling that you are connecting with the earth. How does this feel? Become aware of your body's movement—your arms swinging gently, the position of your head. What can you see and sense?
- Focus on your breathing. In meditation practice, becoming aware of your breathing is a technique that is used to help you be in the moment. If you feel distracted at any point or begin to overthink, simply invite yourself to return to the breath.
- After your walk, you might like to write down your impressions in your Creativity Journal (see page 6).

Why this works
Mindfulness helps to awaken your senses when repetitive activities may leave you feeling shut down and "flat." Giving yourself this type of "slow" time feeds the creative self; it also helps to decrease stress and overthinking, allowing the mind to open up to new possibilities.

The Art OF (GOOD) Boredom

We might feel restless, uncertain, or strangely empty at times: we might tentatively admit to being a little a bit … bored (often confessed in a whisper). Contrary to popular belief, in creativity terms, **periods of inactivity** are certainly not a sign of failure or time wasted. Some boredom is actually essential to the creative process. Enjoying **"non-doing,"** when you can simply "be," **feeds the creative soul**.

A relatively new concept, the word "boredom" was introduced into English in the eighteenth century, at about the same time as the rise in usage of the word "interesting." Boredom was formerly expressed only by the French word *ennui*, and over the years has had many resonances, from a status symbol of the idle rich ("I'm bored, dahling!") to a signifier of failure for today's urban sophisticates who are not entertaining others, or themselves, enough. Boredom has become, strangely, the scourge of modern living, an admission of personal failure, or the finger of blame pointed at substandard entertainment that can't keep us fixated or distracted enough.

As children, we probably remember boredom quite well. Dragged around shopping malls (frustratingly boring) or playing the same old games in the park to fill long summer vacations, we grew up

accepting that boredom was part of living, the bit that made the better parts, like birthday parties, more exciting by contrast. Yet as adults, cultural pressures have made us averse even to admitting that we're a bit bored; in fact, to do so might imply that we are boring. And if we are bored, we'll bore others.

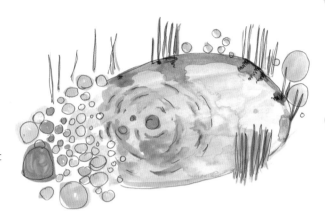

Becoming a bore

Boredom concerned social commentators of the nineteenth century, perhaps most famously the historian and satirist Hilaire Belloc, whose essay *A Guide to Boring* (1931) gives facetious tips on how to "inflict it [boredom] upon our enemies"—as if the Bore were the worst and best kind of social weapon. Here is Belloc's advice:

"It is a very good plan to open with hesitation over a date: 'It was in July 1921—no, now I come to think of it, it must have been 1920, because …' (then tell them why it must have been 1920). 'No, now I think of it, it must have been 1921' (then tell them why it was '21)—'or was it 1922? Anyway, it was July, and the year doesn't matter; the whole point lies in the month.'

"That is a capital beginning, especially the last words, which indicate to the bored one that you have deliberately wasted his time to no purpose."

Yet creativity depends on mild, intermittent boredom, and for this reason, boredom has value; it's not a waste of time, nor does being bored make a bore. Boredom allows you to be yourself in a more relaxed, quietly creative mode. Reducing stimulus to our brain allows us to recharge. Our neural pathways, in their plasticity, are constantly growing and evolving to reflect our experiences. If, for once, we decide to allow ourselves to become a little bit bored, we make room for creative regeneration. We begin to self-entertain— to play, maybe bake, rearrange, daydream, remember an event long forgotten, or muse on what we'd like to be doing. Our observations, along with our rich internal store of memories, experiences, and ideas, are our creative resources, which feed our imagination.

Equally, some people find that boredom makes space for them to be more mindful of the world (see page 41); we can stand and stare, and see things with a renewed sense of wonder. A state of mild ennui can help us to see the value in things we would, when busy, consider insignificant. A visit to the store becomes a sensory, colorful experience rather than a rush in and out on the way to another appointment.

Getting the benefit ... later

In two studies by researchers at the University of Central Lancashire in Preston, England, one group of workers was set the routine task of copying out numbers from a telephone directory for 15 minutes. When they'd finished, they were asked to focus on a creative task—thinking up inventive uses for disposable cups. A control group was given only the disposable cup project. The findings show that those in the first group, who had done the boring task of copying out phone numbers first, were more creative in their cups project than the members of the control group.

In my experience, those who can embrace some boredom without judging themselves often enjoy a creative benefit afterward. It's an important element of the bigger creative process, too. In the nineteenth-century mathematician Henri Poincaré's four stages of creativity (see Chapter 4), the second phase is "unconscious incubation" (which may, or may not, be boring), during which you rest from your project and allow it to grow without your conscious direction. So, in practical terms, at some point in your project you might get bored. Rather than interpret any oncoming boredom as negative, see it as a way for your brain to take a break.

How are you bored?

A study published in the journal *Motivation and Emotion* in 2014 details research by Dr. Thomas Götz and his team at the University of Konstanz, Germany, on five types of boredom:

1 Indifferent boredom—feeling relaxed and indifferent to surroundings
2 Calibrating boredom—feeling uncertain, but open to distraction
3 Searching boredom—feeling restless and searching for distraction
4 Reactant boredom—feeling reactive, or taking action to escape the source of boredom
5 Apathetic boredom—feeling withdrawn, and not wanting change

If something is boring after two minutes, try it for four minutes. If still boring, then eight. Then sixteen. Then thirty-two. Eventually one discovers that it is not boring after all.
JOHN CAGE, *composer*

As I get older, I appreciate reflection and boredom. Boredom is a very creative state.

GRAYSON PERRY, *artist*

In creative work, types 1 and 2 might offer the potential for mild, relaxed boredom that incubates creative ideas; type 3 is the danger zone when we're trying to tune out (see pages 36–37). Type 4 might also be called "frustration" boredom, which usually arises when you're not in control of the boring situation. Extensive studying for exams, being trapped in a place not of your choosing (airport lounge, rail station) or with someone you can't engage with—these are the types of situation that make you fantasize about running away or throwing a bucket of water over the person next to you. Type 5 has only recently been identified, and can be associated with a tendency toward depression.

Embracing good boredom

Mild boredom usually comes with some autonomy; you can choose to stay mildly bored or to distract yourself (particularly if you identify as a type 2 or 3); but always choosing to tune out with computer games, emailing, eating, channel-hopping, or seeking external excitement and stimulation avoids the uncertainty of boredom—and creativity needs uncertainty to thrive. With uncertainty comes the possibility of change.

In the West, we're programmed by advertising and the movie industry to need and expect drama and the promise of entertainment. We're geared to resist boredom. Don't resist; prepare to be bored. Engage with it, and tune in to how it feels. You might even give the word "boredom" a qualifier to make it feel creatively positive, such as "good boredom" or "open time."

- Make space in your diary for unstructured personal time. This is space for you with no allocated tasks. You might feel uncomfortable or even anxious about this concept because you're inviting the possibility of boredom.
- Avoid over-planning. It's tempting to do this when a free weekend yawns ahead, and fill it with back-to-back distractions. But how many times have you liked the thought of busy-ness rather than the reality? When those arrangements come around and it's time to meet friends/go to that concert/have tea with your aunt, you feel more like sitting at home doing nothing. So, before you get busy filling up all your free time, reframe your empty weekend by asking yourself, "What do I not want to do?" And then do as little as possible.
- Daydream. Look at the clouds for a bit and see what you can make out. There may be shapes you like, or that seem to mean something to you.

CHAPTER THREE

Creativity AS A PATH TO Empowerment

For many years, the creative arts have helped us find a path toward **self-acceptance and empowerment**. By writing, telling stories, drawing, moving, acting, and making, we can realize the unique insight our life experience offers. In this chapter, discover how to **create your Personal Vision**, dissolve blocks on the creative journey, and find ways to **tell your life story**—one of the most natural ways to share your creativity with others.

Your PERSONAL Vision

If you have creative hunger and need gentle ways to nurture yourself, you might like to begin by exploring your Personal Vision. A Personal Vision is **an expression of who you are**—your likes and loves, your beliefs and goals. Many people create a focus for their immediate dreams by making **vision boards**, while others work with affirmations that improve the way they perceive themselves. The projects that follow **encourage self-reflection**, and empower you to celebrate the truth of who you are. When you feel connected with your authenticity, ideas flow.

Three ways to create your Personal Vision

Here are three powerful ways to manifest Personal Vision. As well as your imagination, you'll need paper and pen, and magazines and newspapers for the vision board project.

1 Making a vision board

A vision board is a collection of images that mirrors your aspirations and values. Think of five or six things that are important to you: perhaps family, more work or money, a piece of art or craft you'd like to make, a book you want to see published, a partner you'd like to meet, a mentor you value, a famous person you admire. Go through magazines and newspapers, and print out online images. Gather the best representations of what you value and desire, and make a collage on a piece of card or paper. Display it wherever you can see it daily—on your refrigerator or mantelshelf, on the wall of your home office, or in your bedroom.

2 Saying affirmations

Affirmations are short statements that you say ritually to reinforce a particular belief. They work because they program the subconscious mind to generate a positive attitude. Our thoughts create our reality— current research suggests that positive thoughts create new neural pathways in the brain, which become strengthened with habitual use—so habitually good thoughts actually affect the brain's neural networks, also helping to break negative thinking patterns. The word "affirmation" comes from the Latin *affirmare*, meaning to support or strengthen. Write your affirmations on pieces of paper and choose one at the start of each day; you can create your own or, if you like, work with these suggestions:

- I have everything I need to be happy and successful
- Today is the day I make positive changes
- I am always good enough
- Everything is possible

- I am guided to make the best choices for myself
- I love unconditionally
- I can create whatever I desire
- I trust my creativity
- I move forward in the knowledge that I am safe and protected

3 Choosing a "trigger vision"

One of the simplest ways to connect with your goals and values is the "trigger vision." A trigger vision is an everyday symbol that is meaningful to you, and instantly triggers your imagination and positive feelings. For example, business owner Jayne has a rose as her trigger vision: "Every time I spot a rose—from a rose in a garden to a rose logo on a van I happen to be driving behind, I allow myself to imagine love and affection, and when I've imagined it, I actually feel it.

I visualize rose petals, a sweet scent, happiness—a rose makes me feel kind of dreamy and happy whenever I see it. And it seems to get me into a creative zone, somehow—when I need ideas, I'm always in a better frame of mind if I even just imagine my rose."

What's your favorite animal, flower, sport, or color? Visualize it and generate positive feelings around it—for example, a soccer ball and a time when your team won; the color turquoise for the sparkling sea around the Greek island you once visited; or perhaps a black cat, which makes you think of luck and home comforts. Set the intention that you'll notice this trigger vision whenever it arises in your everyday life, and whenever you see it, you'll generate all its positive associations. Then let your imagination fly. (Where else might you swim in a turquoise sea? What sport would you play if you knew you'd be brilliant at it? and so on.)

Why this works

These Personal Vision projects stimulate your imagination and self-awareness. There's no pressure to write or think about other people or external influences. You, alone, are enough.

Dissolving Blocks TO CREATIVITY

The phrase "creative block" is negative in itself, conjuring up the idea of an immovable obstruction that will take the equivalent of a psychological bulldozer to break through. But **the joy of the block** is that it is our own. It is our responsibility, and it is within our power to embrace it, then dissolve it by changing the way we think. A block may come to any creator, and it's an opportunity, every time, to come into a deeper understanding of the self. No ideas? **Unable to start or finish a project?** Welcome to the creative unblocker. See the exercise on the next page to discover whether your subtle attitudes to creativity are blocking your ability to create, then try the suggestions that follow each of the F, R, P, and C profiles. Try not to think too much about each question. Go with your first response each time.

Exercise: "Block" attitudes

Take a look at the statements below and decide which you agree with most strongly, then see the key that follows for the letter (F, R, P, or C) that comes up most often. If you agree with four or more of these statements, it's likely that you are avoiding creative expression. Sometimes we sabotage ourselves rather than deal with the challenges that being creative can bring up.

1. I don't think I was creative when I was younger and I can't learn it now (F)

2. I'll be creative when I've got time, maybe when the children have left home, or we've moved house, or when my job isn't so demanding—creative people don't have all the demands I have to deal with (R)

3. There's no point in trying to make anything because other people do it so much better (C)

4. I just help people with their problems, I'm not creative as such (F)

5. I'm not inspired, I mustn't have the gift of creativity (F)

6. I'm getting too old to do the things I wanted to do (F/R)

7. I can't finish anything I start (F/P)

8. I have very high standards for myself (P)

9. I need money to be creative (R)

In my experience, the biggest blocks to creativity are:

(F) Fear of success, fear of failure, fear of exposure, often expressed as self-judgment

(R) Resentment, in that other people have better circumstances for a creative lifestyle

(P) Perfectionism, often expressed as the inability to finish a project, or the need to delay

(C) Comparison with others

(Julia Cameron, in her brilliant workbook The Artist's Way, *explains in detail ways in which we avoid creative work, from inventing drama and diversions to self-criticism and substance abuse; see the bibliography on page 142.)*

FEAR: DEALING WITH THE SABOTEUR WITHIN

One simple truth is that by trusting ourselves to deal with the risk and reward that creativity offers, we can work through the blocks we put in our way. Being creative can mean taking emotional risks—you are inviting change, which can feel both exciting and uncomfortable. Allow your creative juices to flow and let your dreams take form, and instantly you've created an object, a focus for the attention of other people. We may fear criticism, but often it's our own self-judgment that's the real problem. Some part of us decides to get in there first, sabotaging our fledgling project with negative thoughts before it's even begun. We wouldn't treat a child that way, so begin to consider your creative output as your baby, which needs protection, not criticism.

- Generate a sense of detachment. Observe yourself: while you're creating, imagine a part of you is acting as a witness and appreciating your activity (look, I'm picking up a pen, using some color, stitching, icing, choosing photos ... that's interesting, I like that shade ...). This gives the non-fearful, creative aspect of yourself a voice.

- Trust yourself. You are the best person to be working on this project, and good enough to do whatever you like. Try saying some of the affirmations on page 51.
- Work with some of the Play exercises in Chapter 1 as preparation, to free up your ideas.
- Remember that we are all naturally creative, and we are built this way to benefit our well-being (see Chapter 1). You have an absolute right to create, and to enjoy it.

RESENTMENT: THE MYTH OF THE IVORY TOWER

The perception that creative people live a life detached from society is a romantic ideal that I call the myth of the ivory tower. We might imagine a young, privileged artist in a shabby-chic writing room, about to embark on his next masterpiece. Heeding the call of the Muse, he has all the time in the world to ponder his next verb while his butler tops up his gin and tonic. Or, less imaginatively, you may simply envy someone you know who appears to have more time or money to "indulge" their creative streak. If this resonates with you, you may be exhibiting an attitude of "poverty consciousness"—when you feel time-poor, or cash-poor, or poor in some other way, and that life isn't fair. This sense of deprivation, no matter how well under control, can produce seeds of negativity that grow in the way of your natural creativity.

In order to combat this, you might try:

• Making small changes to your daily routine to make time for creativity; this can have a positive effect on your self-belief (see page 32).
• Being kind to yourself, and seeing the positive aspects of your daily life, by listing your achievements at the end of every day for a week or so, then reflecting on how well you've managed.
• Doing the limitation exercise on page 60 to help you focus.
• Turning negative feelings into creative projects by using any feelings of resentment and anger to tell your life story (see the opposite page).

PERFECTIONISM AND COMPARISON WITH OTHERS

These two creative mind-blocks are often connected: if we're perfect, we protect ourselves from critical feedback and avoid being seen as inferior to others. Perfectionism can be the block that prevents us from finishing a project, but in fact it often conceals a fear of exposure. If your painting, music, writing, quilting, sculpture, or short film is out there in the world, you'll need to deal with how it's received.

Writing or illustrating your life story can help dissolve the blocks of perfectionism and comparison. Creative writing tutor Claire Gillman says: "Telling your story is a safe place to begin creative work, because no one can say what you write isn't true, or criticize it." Here are some ideas on how you might begin.

Exercise: Telling your story

Through stories, we discover the truth of our human experience: just think of the many stories and movies you love because they reinforce your values or your sense of humor, or hold an important message. Many of our oldest stories—fables, fairytales, and parables—hold within them a moral message, expressed through archetypal characters and, often, magical messengers. Little Red Riding Hood should not have left the path in the woods to encounter the talking wolf; Beauty needed to love the handsome prince even when he looked like a beast. There are tales of entrapment and escape in *Rapunzel*, *Hansel and Gretel*, and *Bluebeard*, the jealousy of the ugly sisters in *Cinderella*, and the Little Match Girl's extreme poverty. Reading today's memoirs, we find the same themes: challenge, courage, transformation, and reward. In telling your own story, you write only what you, uniquely, know, while reaching out to others who have shared your experiences.

Reasons to write your memoir

- To "write out" difficult emotions, such as guilt, anger, or loss
- To share extraordinary and ordinary events that have meaning for you
- To make sense of the past
- To record your family history
- To celebrate a family event
  - Because you want to

Here are some ways you might like to tell your story:

Beginnings: go with the feeling

- Start by recalling the part of your life that brings up the most powerful feelings (achievement, sadness, anger, joy …). You might also ask yourself: "What's my darkest thought/fear/belief?"

- Cast yourself as a fairytale character, begin with "Once upon a time," and write in the third person as a way in to writing; as you write more, you may feel comfortable writing in the first person, shifting from he/she/your character into "I."
- Write a little of your story every day, so that writing from your memories becomes a regular part of your present life.
- Memories are stimulated by conversation. Talk to others who share or have shared part of your story, and you may find you begin to remember more.
- Keep a notebook with you and jot down ideas as they come, or record them on your phone. You might begin a scrapbook for memorabilia, or draw what you recall.

TIP: *Guided journals can be a great help when you're starting out. These journals include prompts on each page along with "milestone" pages to fill in, such as "My greatest achievement in my thirties was ...," "My wedding memories," and "Any regrets I have ..."*

Keep a diary

You may or may not have old diaries to lead you back into memories of your earlier years, but regardless, beginning a diary now will help you foster a regular habit of writing and creativity—as well as giving you material for the future. American humorist David Sedaris says: "I've been keeping a diary for 33 years and write in it every morning. Most of it's just whining, but every so often there'll be something I can use later: a joke, a description, a quote."

There's also an intimacy that comes with writing a diary, and the perception that we reveal our secrets to a diary as though to a mute friend. Diaries of the famous and the infamous are uniquely appealing because we sense that we will get a glimpse of the "real" person behind the name. Diarist Anaïs Nin, in her essay "On Writing," comments:

"The diary taught me that it is in the moments of emotional crisis that human beings reveal themselves most accurately. I learned to choose the heightened moments because they are the moments of revelation."

Treat your diary like a confessor: try writing down a few secrets, and get comfortable with disclosing parts of yourself to the page.

Create a collection

Collect material by tracking down old school exercise books, photographs, greetings cards, and diaries. Make a space in your home to gather everything that's connected with your research. Add objects that have sentimental value: a cracked bowl that you mended because it's too precious to discard; a piece of jewelry given to you by a close friend whom you don't see any more; some stones from a beach where you spent a vacation; a leaving card from your old workplace (whatever happened to that guy in accounts you spent four years in meetings with?).

Each object has its own story to tell. Choose one item to act as your springboard into your memories. For example, you might start with a photograph and begin by recalling the circumstances of the photograph, if you were there, or the person or scene it shows.

MAKING ART FROM MEMORIES

Arrange your memory items into themes or a timeline. Display them together, or take photographs of the items and create a montage to frame. Designer Bev Speight custom-makes "memory cubes," collecting from 50 to 2,000 pictures and integrating them into personalized collages. Every little picture shows the person as a baby, child, teenager, at work, with family and friends—all the funny, serious, significant life moments. When the design is done, she has the cube put in Perspex as a permanent tribute to that person. Some clients use her cubes as furniture, so they become very much part of their homes.

THE Gifts OF Limitation

There's a saying that **limitation forces invention**, which was certainly the case for artist Phil Hansen. Nerve damage to his hand meant that he was physically limited in the art he could produce, and through this experience, he learned a valuable lesson about other limitations he could impose upon himself actually to help him create.

Phil used a technique known as pointillism—making hundreds of tiny dots with an ink pen. Years of dotting while he was in high school killed some of the nerves in his hand, leaving him with a permanent tremor and the inability to make round, controlled dot patterns. When his neurologist suggested that he "embrace the shake," Phil changed his technique from dots to loose squiggles, and continued to create amazing portraits.

Later, he got a day job to pay for his art materials, and went crazy in the art store with his first paycheck, buying everything he wanted. But when he got home and tried to make a start, he couldn't do a thing. This situation went on—working at the day job and returning to a home full of art materials in the hope that the creative spark would return. Then Phil thought

back to his neurologist's advice to embrace limitation. He realized that buying loads of art materials and having money meant that he "was paralyzed by too much choice." So he decided on a limitation. He wondered: "What can I create for under a dollar?" He bought a coffee from Starbucks for 80 cents and asked for some free cups, and they offered him 50. Phil made a wall out of the cups, and drew a portrait over the front of them. The limitation idea was working. Next, he thought: "What if I could paint only on my chest?" He created 30 paintings and videoed them. Then, he mused: "What if I could only paint with karate chops?" He dipped the side of his hand in black paint and karate-chopped all over a wall-size piece of paper.

By embracing limitation, Phil recovered his art.

Exercise: Set a limit

Give yourself a zero budget, and see what you can create. Choose your items, perhaps:

• A well-thumbed paperback
• Vintage fabric from a friend
• Found objects to photograph or video, such as feathers, wood, stones
• Used envelopes or shopping receipts
• Ring-pulls from cola cans
• An item you trade

Or try:

• Writing or drawing only with your non-dominant hand
• Painting with your feet or hands (no brush allowed)

Technology can also help us create the limitation that forces creativity. Influential British artist David Hockney used the iPad to create 51 drawings, part of his celebrated project *The Arrival of Spring in Woldgate, East Yorkshire in 2011.* You might like to limit yourself to creating something only on your phone—recording sounds, taking pictures, writing only on the notes app. What possibility does this kind of limitation offer?

The dyslexia connection

Those who have dyslexia and other conditions that limit reading and writing must find inventive ways to work around their disability. Some years ago I was asked to help a friend's daughter, Jas, to read. She was eight years old, and had taught herself to appear to be able to read. She had developed a way of memorizing words and of communicating with classmates to persuade them to let her copy their work, and a confident attitude that hid the fact she couldn't keep up—she possessed a range of life skills in response to her limitation.

Professor Julie Logan, of the Cass Business School at City University London, grew up in a family of dyslexic entrepreneurs. Her research on entrepreneurship and dyslexia shows that 19 percent of UK entrepreneurs are dyslexic (which she says is a "cautious estimate, as we know that some [participants] would not fill in the form"). This is double the rate found in the general population. In her study in the US, she found that one-third of entrepreneurs were dyslexic, which is three times the rate found in the general adult population. She also believes that dyslexics have "an amazing ability to delegate, and fantastic communication skills." As the dyslexic filmmaker Larry Banks says, "we find that the world is not going to go the way we want it to, so we have to keep accepting change and work with that; it becomes an active flow between us and the world."

Telling YOUR Story THROUGH YOUR Home

How many times have you heard the phrase **"If walls could talk"**? Walls—and all the spaces we inhabit—are witnesses of our emotions and experiences. One simple way to begin to express your creativity is to cast your eye over the surfaces of your home. **What does your home say about you?**

In this recent case study, Grace's bare walls had their own healing story to tell.

Grace's walls

I'd known Grace for some years. A teacher and singer, she worked with children in inner-city schools. Her work was stressful, but when she saved enough to buy her first home after a relationship break-up she felt incredibly proud that at last she had her own space. A two-bedroom apartment in a 1930s block overlooking a park, this was the place she could finally call her own. Except it never looked that way. "I just love this place!" she chirruped, pointing out the fantastic city view and the oak trees branching up toward the third-floor apartment. The interior reminded me of a temporary student pad, but I assumed that, over time, it would evolve to feel more homey. Grace wore stunning colors, so I was looking forward to seeing her creativity on the walls, too.

But the décor didn't change. Year after year, the apartment always looked pretty much the same. Cream walls, paperwork covering the one table, a few snapshots stuck to the refrigerator. Grace had begun to buy some shelves and cabinets in order to store her belongings better, but these didn't seem to change the feel of the interior.

Grace wanted a new relationship. A friend of mine, a feng shui consultant, recommended that she designate a section of the main room as a love corner, where she should display objects and pictures evoking love and togetherness—pink or red items, pictures of couples, and ornaments in pairs. So one afternoon we set about trying to find hearts or candles, or old romantic greetings cards. Instead, when rummaging behind the sofa, Grace retrieved a huge, dusty, black portfolio.

"What's in there?" I asked.

"Oh that? It's just my art stuff," Grace sighed.

"Let's have a look," I said, and she spread out huge screen prints, collages, and abstract illustrations in the most amazing colors: deep purple, pillar-box red. It was like looking at the colors of a festival—they were so alive and brilliant.

"These are great, Grace. Did you do them?" I asked.

Grace had been an artist. She told me she had an art degree from a prestigious school. I'd known her for ten years and she'd never mentioned this.

"Why did you stop?" I asked.

"The tutor hated my work. I just knew I'd never be good enough for them … after all, such famous artists studied there and my work was nothing like theirs. I suppose I just gave up … I

scraped through the degree, joined a student band, and that was that."

Nothing in Grace's flat gave any clue to her first love—painting. Because her creativity had not been nurtured by her tutor, she judged her work as not good enough and not worth doing.

"Perhaps you could frame one or two of these?" I suggested.

Two weeks later I returned, and two of Grace's prints had been framed and hung on the walls. Next, she moved her piano keyboard into the main room, and began buying pieces of second-hand furniture, a vintage floor lamp, and some items for her love corner. Yet, in truth, the whole room became an homage to the things she loved: art and music. By showing her creativity openly, on the walls and in the furnishings of her home, Grace had certainly found a new relationship—with her old self.

Who looks outside, dreams; who looks
inside, awakes.
CARL JUNG

Exercise: Does your home reflect you?

Take a look at your home. Walk into each room
with a fresh eye, as if you were a realtor or a new
friend visiting for the first time. What does your
home say about you? Does it reflect your personal
taste, interests, and beliefs? Perhaps your rooms
are crowded with items that reflect the people you
live with—such as children, a partner, or friends.
Maybe the décor is bland because the builder or
landlord chose it. But even if your personal space
is limited or redecorating comes with a level of
restriction, there's always a way for your
personality to shine: in the objects you display and
the pictures you hang on the walls. If you like,
make a list of your observations. If you and your
home feel out of sync, read through the "Block"
attitudes questions on page 54.

Creativity AS Therapy

The use of creative arts in professional therapy began in the 1940s, when psychotherapists and artists first collaborated to work in a non-verbal way with very disturbed clients. Today, **the creative arts are used to help with a range of emotional conditions,** from mood disorder caused by post-traumatic stress disorder (PTSD) to bereavement and dementia.

Someone who has experienced trauma also has gifts to offer all of us—in their depth, their knowledge of our universal vulnerability, and their experience of the power of compassion.

SHARON SALZBERG, *mindfulness meditation teacher and author*

Many dementia sufferers, for example, respond positively to music, which appears to unlock memories that may be unreachable through words in the everyday world. The award-winning US documentary *Alive Inside: A Story of Music and Memory* (2013) follows social worker Dan Cohen as he discovers the power of music to help people with dementia. The film features Alzheimer's sufferer Henry Dryer, age 90-something. Unresponsive to the world and uncommunicative, Henry was given an iPod so that he could listen to his favorite musician, Cab Calloway. With the earphones on, instantly Henry's demeanor changed. He became animated and started to sing along. This level of self-expression continued after the listening session ended, when Henry gave articulate answers to questions about music. When asked: "What does music do to you?" Henry replied, "It gives me the feeling of love." According to neurologist Dr. Oliver Sacks, who is interviewed in the film, Henry "has remembered who he was, has reacquired his identity for a while through the power of music."

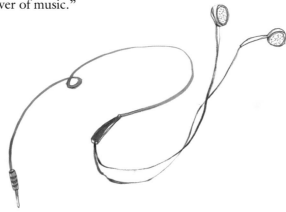

Writing offered the Vietnam War veteran and psychotherapist Larry Winters a way to work through his war experiences. A former director of veterans' treatment at Four Winds Hospital in Westchester County, New York, Larry is also a novelist and a widely published poet. He reflects:

"For my own personal healing concerning PTSD, I found writing poetry to be a step forward in the process of my recovery. It has allowed an internal vehicle to safely plumb my repressed moral struggle after the war … poetry was permission to tell personal truths that would otherwise be seen and judged as diagnostic. After reading Edward Tick's book *The War and the Soul* [2005], I began to understand that morality was affecting my mental health and [that] my poems were a voice of my soul."

Here is Larry's poem "War," which he has kindly given me permission to share:

If a man kills another man
He must dig two graves
One in the earth for the dead man
One in his heart
for his own spirit
Or he will not return.

WAR, LARRY WINTERS

CHAPTER FOUR

Growing YOUR ideas

When we're in a state of **optimal creative flow**, the feeling can be magical—in the "zone," we're completely **immersed in our project**. But how exactly do we get into this mindset? In this chapter, you will discover the steps to the **inspiration flash**, how to shift into the right-brain zone, and how to **flourish through commitment and community**.

How do we Create?

The **French polymath** and philosopher **Henri Poincaré** (1854–1912) believed that the process of creating happens in four phases. To embark on a creative project, we need to start with the **intention to create** (or solve a problem, or achieve some other goal); then we need time to incubate the idea, and let it grow.

Provided we've given ourselves enough time to let our idea bed in without focusing on it consciously, we are rewarded with the inspiration "flash." This is the point of action or realization, when we know what we need to do to make progress. And when we've achieved this, we can finally appraise what we've done.

So, when we're planning to create, we move between conscious and unconscious states of mind, from conscious preparation, to unconscious incubation, to the conscious "flash," followed by conscious evaluation.

Without the unconscious stage—the time to process our ideas internally—it's less likely that we'll be able to create, or complete our creation. The unconscious mind is connected to the right brain (see page 73). By understanding what goes on here, and how to give it space to work, we can fully embrace the creative process.

Poincaré's Four Phases

1 Preparation

The ideas phase, when you might brainstorm or research your creative project, or set about solving a problem using tried-and-tested techniques.

2 Incubation

The phase in which ideas are combined in the unconscious mind when we're doing something else.

3 Illumination (the "flash")

According to Poincaré, this is dependent on the groundwork we've already done: "Sudden illumination [is] a manifest sign of long, unconscious prior work."

4 Evaluation

Appraising your work.

Exercise: Finding inspiration

Here's how to follow Poincaré's four
stages of creativity:

1 **Conscious preparation**
Write down five things that captivate
or inspire you. For example:

- Space exploration
- A lone pilot who circumnavigated
  the world
- The way leaves fall
- Something a child said
- A piece of art that makes you feel
  a certain way

Now make a connection. By this, I
mean work out why that particular
thing inspires you. What is it about
falling leaves, or about a red moon?

Go deeper with this connection. You
might also find yourself connecting
two or more things that come up on
your list. Write them down. You
might want to look at the phrases
in on page 140 and choose two at
random, and see how they might
connect ("cross words" and
"peace"; "music helps" and "finding
answers.") Jot down whatever
springs to mind. If you need to, do
some research—search your memory
or the internet, and talk to people
who can contribute to your idea or
knowledge. Think of this phase as
like baking a cake without a recipe.
You need the ingredients (ideas),
then you must mix them up so they
connect with one another.

2 **Unconscious incubation**
Let your ideas sit for a while. As the
cake needs to bake, so your ideas are
taking form without your conscious
involvement. This might mean
putting your manuscript away for a
week or for months; or just deciding
that you're not going to take any
action on your project just for today.
During incubation, you might

Moving INTO THE Right-brain Zone

cultivate "good" boredom (see page 44) to turn your attention positively to other topics while your creative cake bakes. The important thing is to trust the process.

(3) **The conscious "flash"**
This is the "Eureka!" moment, the point at which the problem is solved, or the idea, or cake, comes together; you suddenly know that what you've made will hold, and/or get a sense of what else you might need to do to make progress. The ingredients have come together to create something original, and now you can identify what it is you've created. The cake's coming out of the oven and, as you greet it, be open to what it might look like. It could be different from what you first imagined.

(4) **Conscious evaluation**
Do you like the cake? Does it look and taste good to your eye and palate? Be generous in your appreciation. Accept what you've made, however it turned out.

The right brain can be perceived as visual and intuitive. According to neurosurgeon Richard Bergland, the right brain "thinks in patterns, or pictures," while the left brain can be understood as rational and analytical, processing thoughts as numbers, letters, and words to form logical sequences. There is some research to indicate that left-handed people are more closely "wired" to specific areas of the right brain, which may indicate that they are more creative.

The artist Dr. Betty Edwards, author of *Drawing on the Right Side of the Brain* (1979), has taught thousands of people to draw using a right-brain approach— including those who had no apparent skill and no experience. It seems that in the right-brain zone, anything is possible. So why do so many of us struggle to access this state of mind?

The creative "crunch"

We experience conflict when we're trying to be creative because our sensible left brains are constantly engaged. This is the part of us that is assessing our creative output as it happens, and unless we can get completely into the right-brain zone, we're constantly switching between left- and right-brain thinking. This switching creates a sense of conflict, doubt, and struggle. The left brain can manifest as the voice that asks how practical your idea is; if it's comparable with others' ideas or output; and if it's good enough. For example, writing fiction while constantly revising previous paragraphs lets the left brain in, constantly interrupting the right brain, which just wants to create, unhindered. Here's a musical example. When reading and playing music, we're using the left brain—interpreting symbols, or notes, into

meaningful sequences through sound. In improvized music, there are no notes, or very few, and musicians are free to play whatever they like. They must tune in completely to the feel of the sound and the sense of the other musicians, and then play something original. If they have to read music and improvize within the same piece, they have to switch modes instantly. Of course, at a professional level this comes with practice, but learning musicians struggle to shift between reading mode and improvising mode; they cannot instantly make the transition and maintain the same standard of playing in both modes. This illustrates the experience of left–right brain clash—the creative "crunch."

You might have a similar experience when sitting in a business meeting going through figures. At the end of the meeting, someone asks for ideas for the theme of the summer party. There's often an ominous silence—this is the sound of the left brain struggling to let go so the right brain can engage, and let ideas and inspiration come through.

If you're "crunching," you may feel:

- Mild anxiety
- Pressure to perform
- Your mind is a blank
- Poor concentration

Exercise: Do the shift

You can spend just a minute on this exercise, or turn it into a longer meditation, depending on how you feel and where you are. With practice, you will be able to do it very naturally, and use it whenever you want to shift gear and de-stress. Many of the other practices in this book will help, too (see Chapter 2 and the mindfulness rituals on pages 42 and 43).

1. Turn your attention from your mind to your body—feel your feet on the floor, the weight of your body in your chair.

2. Move a little. Adjust your sitting position, stretch your neck. This helps release mental intensity and reconnects you with your senses and emotions.

3. Focus on your breathing. In meditation practice, this helps you feel more relaxed and centered. Be aware of your out-breath and try to extend it to a count of five or six, then pause before inhaling. Do this three or four times.

4. Conjure up a favorite image: trees swaying in the breeze, you on a sun lounger; recall a favorite song and sense the vibration of the music; or visualize a color that makes you feel good.

5. Imagine the right side of your brain filling with light, and a little door to your left brain closing. Stay with this image for a few moments.

GETTING Committed

Creative commitment is both attitude and action; when you're not actively working on a project, keep hold of your creative awareness. Take it with you wherever you go, letting it guide you toward opportunities to write, paint, discuss, share, and be inspired.

When you do what you love, it's much easier to commit to it. Without commitment, we never really know if we can succeed. Commitment looks different to different people: for some of you, it might mean committing time, regularly, to your creative project (see page 32 for ideas); for others, talking about your projects with others is a big commitment step. I spent years telling people I'd just met that the books I commissioned were on "mind, body, spirit" subjects, then qualified it by saying "yoga, complementary therapies …," at which they'd nod and agree. The truth was that these were the areas of my work I was least interested in, but I thought they sounded more palatable than the truth, which was that I wrote and commissioned books on spiritual subjects. These days I tell everyone exactly what I do, and if they don't like it, fine—but I generally find that most people respond positively, maybe because they can see that I'm passionate about and committed to my work, and that I don't avoid sharing that. When you feel you're committing time, truth, and energy to your creative projects, it's worth evaluating this commitment as you go along, at each stage of your project.

Entrepreneur Jamal Edwards, author of *Self-Belief: The Vision* (2013), says: "Try anything … The only failure is not trying. And when you find your niche, what you are really good at, hit it so hard." Jamal began making films aged 15. With no formal training and a basic camcorder, he took footage of grime artists he liked and put them on YouTube. He's now a media mogul, making and broadcasting music videos, and an inspiration to thousands of young people.

Miriam's garden

Miriam, a horticulturalist, came to me feeling very frustrated. She'd spent several years writing and illustrating a book on her grandmother's garden, which was one of the finest herb gardens in the country, but had no luck finding anyone to help her publish it.

Our conversation revealed that her idea of finding an agent to represent her meant emailing strangers. In such a competitive market, I explained, this wasn't enough. "But I'm sending it out!" she protested. "It's gone to 20 agents and nearly all so far have said no, or haven't replied at all. What else am I supposed to do?"

I asked her if she had researched the agents she'd contacted, and if she'd considered asking an editorial consultant for feedback.

"No, I haven't. I chose them from a list online. And approaching consultants for advice is expensive."

I asked her to get committed.

"But what does that mean?" she exploded.

"Go into the agents' world. Join a writers' social group that invites agents to speak every month; you'll also get feedback at low cost. Talk to agents, find out what they're interested in and why—research it like you researched your book."

Miriam sighed. "I'm so not a pushy person, though. I can't do that schmooze. Most of the agents I know can tell schmooze a mile off."

"They don't need schmooze, Miriam. They'll respect you for taking an interest in their work."

She looked entirely unconvinced. "I'd just rather keep emailing and hope someone says yes," she muttered.

And there was the fear of exposure and rejection. In her mind, email rejections would almost be easier, as they felt distant. This was also the reason she wasn't making a real connection with the agents. Social media can feed the illusion that we're authentically connected, but it doesn't replace a phone call or a face-to-face conversation.

Staying committed all the way through your project so you can share it means taking the risk and getting intimate—just like beginning a relationship. You have to put yourself in the position of the person receiving your email, and enter their world. I hope Miriam gets the "yes" she's looking for, but I know that a further commitment from her could be the difference between getting noticed in a sea of other talented writers—or not.

YOUR Talents ARE YOUR Material

Your interests, and doing what you love, are the material for any project you'd like to evolve. For some of you, it may be clear already what you love doing. Music may be your thing, or craft, sport, family history: this is all **material for your creative work**. Yet some skills are more subtle, and because of this some people say: "I'm not creative or talented," or "I'm a good all-rounder—I don't know if there is one thing I can do." **Everyone has one or more talents or skills**, whether it's being a good host, caring for others, solving problems, understanding animals, making their home a sacred place, fixing cars, being the family networker, never getting lost, or being able to sail a boat or drive a car.

Exercise: Uncovering your talents

Make a list of your talents. If you're not sure what you're good at, ask a friend or family member to help you. Take one of these skills and apply it to your project. For example, if you're an organizer, apply this to your home (you might be a great organizer at work, but now get de-cluttering and put your house in order, or devise a color scheme for your walls). Write a story about someone like you. Host an event, and think of creative ways your guests can connect (a foodie theme, inviting people whose names begin with A ...). If family history captivates you, make a storyboard of photographs or scanned images into a card for a relative, or turn it into a piece of framed art for your home or to give as a gift. Write a poem about the life you imagine one of your ancestors had. Find a way to visit an area where your relatives once lived; take photographs. Embroider a family tree.

Become an expert on yourself, and know what lights your creative fire. When you're doing what you love, you're entering a state of creative flow.

How to know when you're in the flow
Being in the flow is a state of mind. Here are some of the ways you might experience flow:

- You feel immersed and engaged
  - The work feels spontaneous
  - You can't not do what you're doing
  - You're unaware, or less aware, of time
  - You feel happy/excited/content/complete
- You feel motivated to make a meaningful contribution

Read more about the happiness and play attributes of creativity in Chapters 1 and 2.

FEEDING THE FLOW:
FROM Pairing Up TO Finding Community

Many successful businesses are based on **partnership**. From Barnes & Noble, Rolls-Royce, and Laurel and Hardy to Lennon and McCartney and Dolce & Gabbana, they all began with two people having a conversation, and **deciding to work together** rather than alone.

Collaboration feeds creativity, helping us make new connections, push boundaries, and reach beyond our individual interests. Creative pairs often complement each other, pooling their own unique skills and perspectives, and so a creative partnership can be greater than the sum of its parts. However, social media makes it possible to go beyond the traditional pairings and communicate with networks of fellow creatives for feedback, support, and stimulation. You can brainstorm ideas with kindred spirits on innovation sites such as IdeaScale. Alternatively, investigate crowdfunding for your project by using a crowdfunding website to attract backing from the public, who get to be involved with the project as it progresses (check out sites such as Crowdfunder, ArtistShare, and Kickstarter). Crowdfunding has been used to attract individual contributions toward scientific research, environmental initiatives, movie-making, video games, music, and products from customized watches to skateparks or graphic novels. It supports both new ventures and established artists who want to avoid traditional routes to market. In 2005, American composer Maria Schneider won a Grammy music award for her ArtistShare release *Concert in the Garden*; and musician Amanda Palmer, formerly of the Dresden Dolls, raised over $1 million through Kickstarter to fund her album *Theatre is Evil* (2012).

Today, authors and artists can have a direct connection with their readers through social media, and some are using this as a way to invite their fans to be part of their projects and to develop a broad, loyal fan base, without investing money. English author Silvia Hartmann wrote her fantasy novel *The Dragon Lords* (2012) live in Google Docs, so fans could see her writing in real time and give feedback about the plot and characters as the story progressed. And in 2014 the award-winning English novelist David Mitchell, author of *Cloud Atlas* (2004) and *Ghostwritten* (1999), took to Twitter to share his new short story, *The Right Sort*, in 367 tweets.

Exercise: The creative hook-up

(1) Partner with a friend, acquaintance, or social-media contact who works in a different discipline—for example, if you bake, hook up with a writer; if you like fashion, pair up with a poet. Come up with an idea together in a week, beginning with a conversation over coffee or a glass of wine. What would you like to make together? Share your interests. Your collaboration is about making connections, sensing how one discipline can feed another. Cake story? A poem inspired by Coco Chanel's sunglasses?

(2) Put your ideas out on social media: look for groups that share your interests, and ask for creative companions to brainstorm with.

CHAPTER FiVE

CREATiVE Problem-Solving

No matter what issues you face, there are **limitless creative ways to think outside the box**. This chapter offers tried-and-tested strategies, from **brainstorming**, **mind-mapping**, and **tapping**, through lateral thinking and linking with past success to **break through blocks** and find solutions. You can apply all these techniques to kickstarting a new project, too.

A Change of Attitude

A **creative mindset** benefits all aspects of our being: mood, self-direction, openness to learning, and, perhaps above all, a sense of feeling truly present and connected with our environment, so we are conscious of every moment. A creative approach can become our daily attitude. It can help us to see life, and its challenges, in a new light. We begin to think differently, in terms of **"What if I did this that way?,"** and to recognize the opportunities a challenge can offer, rather than framing it as a negative block.

The fact that there are so many different ways to solve problems, particularly in business coaching, suggests that there's a problem with applying logic—that following steps A, B, and C doesn't always get us to where we want to be. While we do need to be able to assess our ideas in a logical way, we must first let our imagination run free, without judgment, to break away from given patterns and see new solutions and alternatives.

Begin WITH THE Brainstorm

Brainstorming suggests creative chaos, a literal storm within the mind. Ideas are blown about, new concepts spiraling in the sky, tornado-style … but I'm getting ahead of myself here. In business, the brainstorm often requires participants to sit round a boardroom table and throw phrases up into the air or at one another. The term is associated with advertising executive Alex Faickney Osborn, who felt the need to find more creative ways to generate advertising ideas for his clients. He organized groups of workers to contribute any ideas they liked, and discuss them in a group, pooling a whole lot of concepts, discussing them, and selecting some for development.

Brainstorming, however, also works for individuals, and is perhaps even more effective if you're doing it alone with just your paper and pen (a study in 2006 by Helmut Lamm and Gisela Trommsdorff found that brainstorming in a group may actually be limited by social inhibition). Here's how to get the best from your own brainstorming session.

Brainstorming involves:

- Gathering ideas, and drawing them or writing them down as you go
- Including all the possibilities, no matter how random
- Using free association
- Letting ideas flow without self-judgment
- Making new connections between ideas

Exercise: The lone brainstorm

First, get some positive energy flowing for a few minutes—sketch, play your favorite music, or think of a mentor or celebrity you admire: generate a happy feeling. Next, set a time limit. This is the length of time you will put ideas to paper. After your allocated time is up, your unconscious mind will continue to process and formulate ideas when you start doing something else—washing dishes, walking to work, having a meeting on an unrelated topic, so there's no pressure to generate solutions immediately.

The Brainstorm

• Take a large piece of paper—don't restrict yourself with a small page as this suggests your ideas have to fit a limited space. Write down your goal or dilemma in the center of the paper.

• In pictures and/or words, put down whatever comes into your mind around the goal/dilemma. Move fast and keep going. Don't assess your work at this stage.

• When you've finished, take a break. Do something else.

TIP: *Imagine that your pen is connected to your mind. Your hand is just a tool to get the ideas down.*

Review

• Later, review your work—what ideas do you respond to the most? Which ones give you a buzz? Some might surprise you.

• Give your brainstorming work a title and a date. If you like, fold it up and staple it in your Creativity Journal (see page 6) for future reference.

Exercise: Brainstorm with free writing

For this exercise, you'll need a pen and your Creativity Journal (see page 6) or a notebook. Don't use your computer—you need to feel the connection between your hand and the words.

• Write two pages, using a phrase to get you started, such as "Today I'm feeling as though I might …." Don't read what you've written yet. You might find yourself wanting to write out clutter first, beginning with to-do lists or shopping lists, to get immediate worries out of the way so that unconscious creative ideas can come through.

• Write quickly, and don't pay attention to spelling or grammar (this might be a challenge if you're a pedant about the use of the apostrophe, or if you're used to editing what you write as you go). This can feel quite exposing at first, as if you're writing like a child, focusing only on the idea or the story. But writing without worrying about punctuation and correct spelling keeps your right brain engaged, without allowing the left brain to jump in and assess what you're doing—which can hinder the creative flow.

TIP: *This is also a great way to work through procrastination and other blocks (see page 90 and Chapter 3), and it's a technique used by many creative-writing teachers to get students into the flow of ideas without stopping to self-assess.*

Mind-mapping

The mind map is a focused method of looking at ways to work toward goals and solutions. It takes the form of an image that reflects your **thoughts**, **associations**, and **ideas**, and shows how they might connect, helping you see paths to your goals and break through problems. The brainchild of neuro-linguistic programming pioneer **Tony Buzan**, mind maps can help you see new, creative ways to approach any situation. While there are courses run by Buzan on detailed ways to mind-map, here's a taster exercise to show how you might begin to create your own maps and untangle daily challenges.

Exercise: The wordless mind map

Begin by drawing your main goal in the center of a large piece of paper. Now draw branches coming off it, placing other ideas on the branches, then adding sub-branches for less important ideas or associations. Link any connected task with a line. Your mind map may look something like the one above.

Next, look again at the goal you've drawn in the center. Now assess all the branches, and delete those that don't directly support your goal. This should leave you with only the actions and ideas that will create the outcome you want.

Why this works

By working with pictures rather than words, you connect with the creative right brain. When you assess your picture, you're using your logical left brain, judging the content and editing down the tasks. Follow your mind map, and you'll be able to work more effectively to unravel a problem, or to shape your project or idea.

Fifty–five–five:

HOW TO USE AN HOUR TO

Find a Solution

One of the reasons problem-solving is beset with anxiety is that so many problems come with a deadline. When panic to meet the deadline sets in, **we feel blocked** and pray for the lightbulb moment, for the answer to appear in a flash of inspiration. If you're suffering from **deadline anxiety**, stop, take a breath, and try this approach.

What you need to do is actually quite simple: investigate the cause of the dilemma rather than feeling pressed to find a solution now. Albert Einstein famously said: "If I had an hour to solve a problem I'd spend 55 minutes thinking about the problem and five minutes thinking about solutions." Here are some ways in which you might turn detective. You can set 55 minutes for your investigation, or have open-ended time—the point is to spend proportionally longer considering the problem that being solution-driven:

- Is the problem yours to solve? Have you taken it upon yourself to resolve something you didn't create?
- What opportunities does the problem offer? For example, might it lead you to think in new ways or break new ground—or will you gain benefit or a reward when the problem no longer exists?
- Check your language. Is there negativity or/and pressure in the questions you're asking yourself? Try rephrasing the problem in a more positive light. For example, "How do I get this essay/report written now?" could be rephrased as, "What's the best approach I can take to this work now?"
- Break it down and get some distance. Break down the problem into chunks and name each chunk, then draw a box naming each one. This helps you to define the elements of the problem while creating some distance between yourself and it. Then draw boxes for all the possible solutions you can think of, and brainstorm as if it's not your problem.

Imagine that you're helping another person, and are offering them creative solutions.

- Check your assumptions. Can a deadline change? Is a contract irrevocable? Can you break the rules? Cancel an agreement? If a situation is causing far too many problems, investigate if there will be enough reward in the long term to warrant you solving the problem that's been created.
- Change your environment. Changing your environment helps you alter your perspective (see the exercise on page 92).

When you've done your investigative groundwork, spend your last five minutes (or any time you allocate) on deciding what action to take to break through the problem. Make the decision. If you're procrastinating and can't see a way forward, try the tapping exercise on page 100.

Exercise: Take your problem for a walk

Taking a "thought walk," a phrase coined by the eighteenth-century philosopher Jean-Jacques Rousseau, is a time-honored tradition among creative people, helping them to think, plot, dream, and problem-solve; Charles Dickens walked to ruminate, as did Mark Twain and Sigmund Freud.

• Set an intention to take your problem with you and give it some air. Go for a walk at your usual pace, then begin to slow down. Run through all the possible scenarios attached to your problem as if you're running a mini-movie in your mind. Now visualize that the movie is still running, but at the back of your mind, rather than in front of you. Begin to observe what's going on around you.

• What you notice on your walk can be metaphors for new approaches and solutions. For example, roadworks might suggest that you need to cordon off the part of the problem that causes most disruption, and ask experts (like the maintenance crew you see) for support. You might link the pigeons fighting over breadcrumbs with you and the management structure in your company, or gain perspective on your dilemma when you see a child enjoying an ice cream. Make the connections between the problem and the external world. What you notice can unlock solutions and inspire you to think differently.

Why this works

Moving our bodies through walking seems to move stuck dialogue, while the new places we see on our walks offer new perspective on old problems.

I can only meditate when I am walking. When I stop, I cease to think; my mind only works with my legs.
JEAN-JACQUES ROUSSEAU

THE introvert–extrovert
SWITCHOVER

Are you an extrovert or an introvert? **Here's a quick test**: do you recharge by being alone (introvert), or feel energized by being with other people (extrovert)? Spending one day practicing the behavior of your "opposite" mode gets you out of your comfort zone, helping you to see a problem with a **fresh perspective**.

Exercise: inside out

If you're naturally an introvert, try behaving like an extrovert for one day. Plan a day that will take you into maximum contact with people: store up phone calls to return; shop with the intention to communicate with assistants; use public transport.

If you're naturally an extrovert, try behaving like an introvert for one day. Avoid talking to people. Stick to essential emails and texts only, and do this first thing in the morning. Then switch off your phone; avoid the compulsion to communicate. This is time just for you, to make space for your own ideas. Stay home, or walk alone. Read; think; look out of the window.

At the end of the day, return to your problem. What new insights do you have?

EXTROVERT QUALITIES

- Focuses on what's going on outside the self

- Discloses personal information easily

- Natural networker: has close friends, but is excited by meeting new people; has a wide circle of contacts

INTROVERT QUALITIES

- Focuses on the internal world

- Needs privacy

- Small friendship groups; needs few friends to be happy

Read: *Quiet: The Power of Introverts in a World that Can't Stop Talking* (2013) by Susan Cain.

Linking
IN TO PAST experience

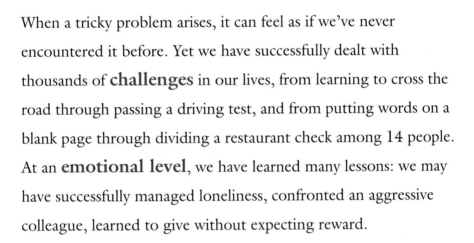

When a tricky problem arises, it can feel as if we've never encountered it before. Yet we have successfully dealt with thousands of **challenges** in our lives, from learning to cross the road through passing a driving test, and from putting words on a blank page through dividing a restaurant check among 14 people. At an **emotional level**, we have learned many lessons: we may have successfully managed loneliness, confronted an aggressive colleague, learned to give without expecting reward.

Think back and identify what you consider to be your greatest tests and achievements, those that give you the strongest feelings. How did it feel when you achieved your goal? Generate that feeling of breakthrough, and give it a name, for example:

- Quitting a bad habit: "fresh air" for smoking, "confident me" for losing weight.

- Successful creative projects: "gold star," "fulfillment".
- A life-changing conversation: "words with XX or about XX event".
- Recovery from illness: "freedom," "pain-free," "happy–healthy".

Use these words as triggers when you need reminding of your past success; this will help you feel confident about your ability to solve a present dilemma. Imagine you have a fishing rod, and you're fishing out your feel-good phrase. Allow the phrase to connect with the positive feeling you experience. Write down your achievements. You might find that you remember occasions that got buried. You might begin with your obvious successes, then unearth something deeper, more rewarding.

Ahmed's solution

Ahmed, a computer programmer, tried this memory technique when he was posed with a complex problem at work. He had to devise workflow schedules for more than 40 staff, and, after several failed attempts, even toyed with trying to avoid the task altogether (although he hadn't yet thought how he might explain this to his boss). The more he ignored the work he'd been set, the more oppressive it felt, like a bad-tempered dog skulking in the corner of his office.

Ahmed took a break and thought about his past problem-solving achievements. There hadn't been too many, but he listed them. At the bottom of the list he saw he'd written down the name "Ali." He recalls:

"My friend Raj had told me that his eight-year-old son, Ali, was struggling to read. I said I'd drop by and read with him, as I was working part-time and could spare a few hours a week. But in the first session, I realized I had a real problem on my hands, and I didn't know how to help him. Raj

knew I wasn't a teacher, but he was adamant I could help. Ali read aloud to me, but it was clear he'd memorized most of the words. He struggled with the phonetics, but seemed to know some things rather than others, so I couldn't pinpoint exactly where the problem lay. And he got bored easily, too. I didn't feel we were making any progress. But one thing Ali loved were comics, so we read those together just to keep his interest.

"Then I decided to work with the comics, and asked him to go through a page with a highlighter pen, highlighting just the letters 't' and 'd.' From this, I learned what he could and couldn't do, and we worked on filling his knowledge gaps.

"Slowly, Ali began to learn, always from his comics. After two months, I'd learned a lot about Spiderman, while Ali wrote a story for his dad and read it to him. What I felt after remembering this was not only that I could solve a problem—and help someone solve theirs—but that what had worked was keeping it simple. Ali had learned to recognize a regular pattern by finding the same letter over and over again. I began to think that I'd made my current problem more complex than it needed to be. So I tried pulling together all the elements of my program that shared similar properties to create the workflow spreadsheet. I didn't get a 'Eureka' moment, but slowly I began to get a grip on what I needed to do to move toward a solution."

Oblique Strategies:
OVER 100 WORTHWHILE DiLEMMAS

Brian Eno and his friend the painter Peter Schmidt created 100 cards, each with a printed message, to inspire lateral thinking. Lateral thinking, first described in 1967 by the doctor and author Edward de Bono, is an approach that uses creative, indirect ways to stimulate solutions, rather than using imagination or step-by-step logic.

The Oblique Strategies deck is most associated with Eno's approach to creative music-making, as he famously used the cards when working as a writer and musician with David Bowie on Bowie's classic albums *Low*, *Heroes* (both 1977), and *Lodger* (1979), and more recently with Coldplay on their album *Viva La Vida* (2008). The cards can be used to help solve many problems in business, too.

Chosen at random, the cards' messages are not considered final solutions or direct instructions, but rather prompts to find alternative ways of thinking—particularly when you're working under pressure. Eno says:

"If you're in a panic, you tend to take the head-on approach because it seems to be the one that's going to yield the best results. Of course, that often isn't the case... The function of the Oblique Strategies was, initially, to serve as a series of prompts which said, 'Don't forget that you could adopt *this* attitude,' or 'Don't forget you could adopt *that* attitude'."

Each card has a statement or a question, such as:
"Tidy up"
"Destroy: Nothing."
"Destroy: The most important thing."
"Who should be doing this job?"
"How would they do it?"

There are 100 cards in the deck, but you can make your own with fewer messages. The trick is to make the subjects of the messages as diverse as you can, by choosing them randomly from a range of sources.

Exercise: Making Oblique Strategies cards

Source material:

• Use the word and phrase lists on page 140.
• Take a favorite novel or a dictionary. Flick through the pages, stop at random, and choose statements, speech, or one word and write it down.
• The internet: use the word "proverb" or "quotation" as a search term, and click on one of the results at random. Or pick a news story and choose the tenth and fifteenth words or phrases from the first sentence or paragraph. If you have a lucky number, use this to pick your messages. Keep it random.

Also, you could try the same method using:

• A self-help book
• A cookbook
• Poetry
• A newspaper or magazine
• A nugget of overheard conversation

Write each message on a blank card, about the size of a business card (you can buy these online), leaving the reverse of the card blank. Keep the cards in your desk drawer or purse, and when you need to make a decision or solve a difficult problem, take five minutes with your cards and draw one or more at random, face down. Then see how your card message(s) offer an alternative approach.

Tap on a Problem

Tapping, also known as Emotional Freedom Techniques, involves tapping on eight acupoints on the body in sequence while saying aloud a phrase that describes the problem and its associated feelings. The tapping action helps the energy field to function correctly, and may also increase levels of serotonin, the body's happiness chemical. Tapping has had lots of success treating phobias, post-traumatic stress disorder, performance anxiety, and physical pain, and tackling addiction, helping people to quit smoking and lose weight. It's based on an exposure therapy known as Thought Field Therapy, developed by the psychologist Dr. Roger Callahan. Exposure therapy lessens the threat of a problem through exposure to it. In tapping, a problem is repeated out loud so that the brain recategorizes it as less threatening or non-threatening, helping remove the anxiety associated with it and "clearing" the emotions. Because of the neuroplasticity of the brain, it's believed that tapping helps build new neural pathways, so that when the anxiety or danger are experienced again in the future, we don't react to them so negatively. In this way, tapping has helped thousands of people to break free from habitual thinking patterns.

Tapping points

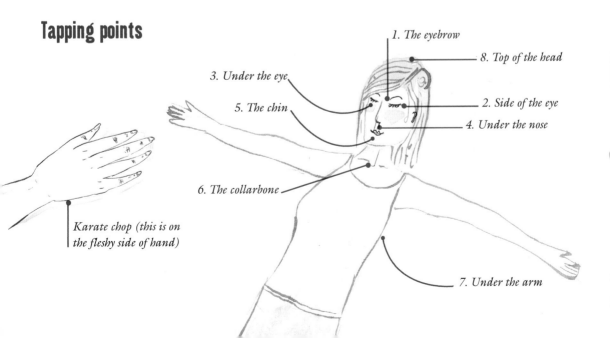

1. The eyebrow
8. Top of the head
3. Under the eye
5. The chin
2. Side of the eye
4. Under the nose
6. The collarbone
7. Under the arm

Karate chop (this is on the fleshy side of hand)

99

Exercise: How to tap through any problem

- Begin by identifying what's bothering you the most. It might be the pressure to complete a task, or confusion, or perhaps feeling overwhelmed with too much to do. How big is it on a scale of 1–10? How intense does it feel? Rate its intensity on a scale of 1–10, too. The idea is that the rating will drop as the tapping progresses; many people say that tapping brings them a sense of peace and wisdom.

- Now say your problem out loud: "complex problem," "low energy," "angry with boss," etc.

- Tap on the karate-chop point and say the "set-up" statement out loud: "Even though I have this [problem], I completely and deeply love and accept myself." For example: "Even though I have these anxious feelings, I completely and deeply love and accept myself." Say the set-up statement three times as you tap five to seven times.

- Shorten your set-up statement to a brief reminder phrase. For example:
  SET-UP STATEMENT: "Even though I have this feeling that I can't move forward, I completely and deeply love and accept myself."
  REMINDER PHRASE: "Can't move forward."

- Say the reminder phrase out loud as you tap on each of the eight points five to seven times. When you've finished, take a deep breath and assess how you feel on the scale of 1–10.

- Now repeat. As you tap on the different points, keep tuning in to how you feel. You may find other feelings coming up, and you might adapt your reminder phrase as you go to reflect them. So:
  Eyebrow: "This problem."
  Side of eye: "This problem, it's difficult."
  Under eye: "Difficult, stress problem."
  Under nose: "Stress problem."

Chin: "Stress, tight in my stomach."

Collarbone: "This tightness."

Under arm: "Tightness, fear feeling."

Top of head: "This fear."

Take a breath, and assess the intensity of the problem
on the 1–10 scale.

• Repeat one more time, and again rate the problem from 1–10.

In summary:

• Rate the problem on a scale of 1–10.

• Say your set-up statement three times while tapping on the
karate-chop point.

• Do three rounds of tapping on the eight points. Say your
reminder phrase once on each of the points.

• At the end of each round of tapping on the points, take a deep
breath, then rate yourself between 1–10. With each round, you
may see the rating drop.

You can continue doing more tapping rounds, going deeper
into the feeling associated with your problem, and
changing your script to explore it. If you
want to find out more, many excellent books are
available explaining how tapping affects the body,
along with suggested scripts for different problems
(see page 142).

Tap away procrastination

As jazz musician Joe Venuti said, "If you're going to make a mistake, make it loud so everybody else sounds wrong." Procrastinators generally prefer not to make it loud—to be decisive—but, as a result, they can miss out on the lessons of failure. Many entrepreneurs, including Henry Ford, H. J. Heinz, and Richard Branson were bankrupts before they gained the experience and knowledge to run a successful business. If we do nothing, all we learn is the art of procrastination.

Tapping can help with procrastination, as it works on lowering the anxiety that procrastinators often feel. If this is a problem for you, try the exercise on the opposite page (maybe; maybe not. You decide).

Exercise: The procrastination script

Begin by rating yourself on the 1–10 scale (see page 100).
Then devise your set-up statement, which might be:
"Even though I can't get going on this project, I completely
and deeply love and accept myself."

Or:
"Even though I keep getting distracted …"
"Even though I can't make up my mind …"
"Even though I feel stressed at the thought of …"

Tap this statement on the karate-chop point three times.
Then devise your reminder phrase, which might be:
"Distracted …"
"Stressed at the thought …"
"Can't decide …"

Now tap on the eight points in three rounds, assessing how you
feel on the scale of 1–10 after each round.

What insights did you gain?

It was my fear of failure that first kept me from attempting the master
work. Now, I'm beginning what I could have started ten years ago. But
I'm happy at least that I didn't wait twenty years.
PAULO COELHO

CHAPTER SIX

CREATIVITY AND INTUITION: YOUR Creative Sixth Sense

Intuition is the voice of the authentic self, the truth about ourselves that we hold within. When we are able to listen to this voice, the benefits are immense: fulfillment, protection, love, empowerment—and creativity. In this chapter, discover how to **heighten your sensitivity** to develop your intuition, how to use intuition's magic words, how to **meditate to invoke your muse**, and how to link in to the intuition frequency with oracle cards. You will be intuitively drawn to the stories and exercises that are perfect for you now.

Becoming intuitive

Intuition is our inner knowing, an innate wisdom that may run contrary to accepted logic and rational thought. When we follow our intuition, we trust the truths we sense within. Acting on intuition not only benefits our creative projects, but all life areas. It keeps us on the right path, protects us from potential hurt, or senses opportunity and propels us toward it. Intuition tells us when to say yes and when to say no. And if we don't heed those messages first time around, intuition is forgiving. It returns, again and again, nudging us until we listen.

HOW FAMILIARITY BREEDS INTUITION

Self-employment guru and author Patrick Schwerdtfeger believes that intuition can be developed when we immerse ourselves in a situation. The more we expose ourselves to a particular environment, the more chance the unconscious mind has to organize its millions of observations into patterns, allowing us to become more intuitive. He gives examples of experienced soldiers looking down a street and knowing, without any obvious signals, that a bomb is there, and drivers sensing exactly when the car in front is going to change lane before that car has moved or even indicated. Experience, therefore, supports our intuition. If we take this observation into the realm of creativity, it suggests that the more familiar we become with taking creative approaches in our daily lives, the more our intuition builds.

No matter how intuitive you believe you are, intuition can be developed. By connecting more with your senses—the receptors of intuition—you can allow your intuition to be felt. It might manifest as excitement and a feeling of anticipation when you're in creative flow; an inexplicably good feeling about a person you've just met; or anxiety or a dull, unsettled sensation in the pit of the stomach when a situation just doesn't feel right (although your logical left brain is telling you that everything should be okay). Alternatively, you might hear an intuitive voice giving an instruction. We can identify two types of intuition:

Direct intuition The signs may be obvious: for example, your body takes over and starts walking one way when you had decided to take another route; or you hear a voice with an instruction. Many survivors of disasters report experiencing direct intuition, such as voices or a flash image that led them to safety.

Indirect intuition You might see symbols or situations in dreams and wake with a strong feeling that you are meant to pay attention (rather than having a "processing" dream, a mash-up of the previous few days' events). Or, an indirect message can occur as a general feeling of malaise; you sense there's something "off," but are unsure what it means or what action to take. In this case, pay special attention to how you respond in your body to different situations, and see if you can sense a pattern associated with this feeling—for example, when you're in contact with a particular person, or reacting to a routine task.

The creativity connection

Intuition and creativity function in the right brain, the zone of emotions, dreams, the unconscious, and symbols. Studies show that the unconscious mind can make about 10 million observations in a given setting, while the conscious mind can make anything between 40 and 150 observations—which means that we're not consciously aware of 99.99 percent of what's going on.

An intuitive feeling and a creative impulse often occur in similar circumstances, and share similar attributes. Here are just a few examples of how intuition often manifests; you may find that you experience creativity in similar ways:

- Intuition strikes when we don't expect it; it's often instant.
- It doesn't always fit with your plans or expectations.
- Intuition is felt through your senses.
- You may get intuitive messages in dream.
- Intuition likes quiet moments, when the left brain is not busy: times of reflection, meditation, or prayer.
- The ability to follow intuition may be blocked by fear, doubt, or low self-esteem.
- An intuitive message (a feeling, a knowing) keeps coming back if at first you don't follow it.
- When you follow your intuition and take action, there's a sense of relief and/or reward.
- The more you follow your inner knowing, the more content you feel; life becomes better.

Exercise: Four ways to awaken the senses

To strengthen our intuition, we need to tune into our senses and the rich territory of the unconscious mind. Use your intuition to choose the exercise that's right for you by skimming the exercise headings in bold and choosing the one that immediately feels right. Don't think about it—just respond to your inner knowing.

* **Connect with nature.** Walk outdoors or sit in your yard or on your terrace or balcony if this is a peaceful space for you, and if it has plants and/or trees. Rather than purely observing what's around you, choose something to touch: the bark of a tree, a leaf, a cold park railing. You might pick up a scent (mown grass, candy, damp dog). Touching and scenting in this way will ground you in the here and now. Being present to your environment heightens your senses. Notice the people around you. Are they really here, too—or on their phones, distracted?

* **Find quiet time.** This might be on your walk above, or a few moments

at home when you can sit in stillness. Close your eyes and focus just on the sound of your breath and the movement in your body: your shoulders rising and falling, the feeling of your lungs filling with air and then letting go. Visualize your mind emptying, as though water is flowing out of a pitcher. Keep the focus on your senses, and become aware of every sensation you feel. Let sensation fill you up. You might sense a color, a feeling, a knowing.

* **Listen to music.** Choose a track that reminds you of a joyful occasion. This time, when you listen, focus on one aspect of the music—perhaps the bassline, melody, or accompaniment— tuning in to each note and its rhythm. See if you can notice something in the music you haven't heard before. If you can play a musical instrument—piano, recorder, harmonica, whatever—play it, or just drum out a rhythm on your desk.

* **Hold an object** that is meaningful to you for a minute or two—a piece of jewelry or other keepsake, or a stone you brought home from the park or beach

that connects you with the positive experience you had in that place. You might like to hold a crystal such as labradorite or amethyst, for intuition, or turquoise, for communication. Feel the surfaces of your object and begin to sense its subtle vibration in your palm.

Why this works
Connecting to our senses through the body helps us step out of thinking mode into feeling mode, tapping into our unconscious knowing. When we become more present to our senses through our body, we open up a communication pathway to our intuition.

Trust:
THE KEY TO HONORING YOUR
Creativity
AND intuition

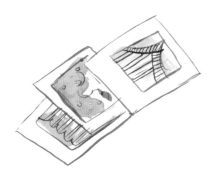

In creative work, one essential quality links the creative process with intuition. To be **creative** and to follow our intuition, we must **trust** ourselves.

When we don't trust our intuition or our ability to create, we disconnect ourselves from one of our most precious internal resources. It's rather like finding an orchard brimming with ripe fruit— the instant solution to your hunger—looking longingly at it, then immediately withdrawing the hand that reaches out to the branch. It can't be true, can it? Not only that the orchard exists, but that you found it naturally, without meaning to. You look at your map and walk away, because according to the map, it's not supposed to be there at all. It's not been written down, validated by a cartographer, or visited by anyone else but you. Yet we are raised on fairytales, stories that offer us magical possibilities and are full of heroes

and heroines who don't conform. Red Riding Hood drifts from the path and into the lair of the wolf, but in doing so discovers the danger her grandmother had been in all along. Eventually, the wolf is killed by the woodman, and Red Riding Hood and her grandmother are saved. Bluebeard's bride is told never to go into the bloody chamber, but of course she does, and discovers the corpses of his previous brides—and learns what would have been her own fate, had she not turned the key. As children, we see heroes straying—following their intuition— and they are still rescued, wiser for the experience. Yet as adults we can too easily leave behind the magical possibility that our intuition is right. And even when we are aware that our intuition is beginning to shout, we can delay taking action.

The creative–intuitive link

Many people who feel blocked intuitively are also blocked at a creative level. If we suppress our intuition, which comes from the unconscious, we may suppress our creativity, too.

Ann, a photographer, describes this feeling as losing her "inner compass." "I'm doubting everything I feel now," she explained to me, "and I feel like I've lost a part of me, but I don't know why." It transpired that Ann needed to make a decision that would disrupt her life considerably. Her intuition was telling her to leave her relationship, but she didn't want to listen, and tried, instead, to think positively about how to fix it. This situation had gone on for several years, during which time her work had begun to suffer, too: "I've put so much into my marriage that I now don't have an idea in my head." Ann had been offered a major photographic exhibition, but, as she explained, "I'm just not good enough to do it. I might have to refuse."

The thing about intuition, like creativity, is that it refuses to go away. We might placate it by saying "One day I'll write my book, leave my relationship, date again, learn Italian," but if we don't take action, that nagging feeling keeps returning; and the same unfulfilling patterns get repeated. If you look back on your life, you might relate to this: a job or relationship that limped on for years. You always knew you had to leave—your intuition told you. But intuition can be very inconvenient. It's great when our inner knowing guides us toward an opportunity or gives us a good vibe about a particular person, but it can be harder to take the leap of faith when the intuition message means a whole lot of disruption. But sometimes, the difficult decisions can be the only way forward if we're to follow our life path—the life we should be living for ourselves, not for anyone or anything else. And the rewards of following the difficult intuition prompts can be immense.

Ann came back to me three months later. She'd decided to take a break and live separately from her partner for a while, until they could see where their relationship might go. This had been a big step, but, as Ann said, "it's given me some safe distance to see how I feel." On reflection, she decided to accept the exhibition offer and had made a start on a new project, traveling away from her hometown to research and photograph new subjects. By finally paying attention to her intuition, she had allowed her natural creativity to flow once again. While this didn't mean everything was perfect, she had begun to see a way forward, a way to start feeling like her familiar creative self.

intuition AND Messages
FROM THE Body

If we don't pay attention to our **intuition** for a long time, it tries to give us its **message** through an ailment.

Here are some of the ways that our inner knowing can show up in the body to express its "dis-ease"—when we are not at ease with our intuition:

Problems with legs and feet   *Fear of moving forward*

Lower back problems   *Feeling unsupported; financial problems*

Shoulder ache   *Feeling burdened; too much responsibility*

Headaches   *Overwhelm; too much to think about*

Indigestion   *What you can't digest*

Earache   *You don't like what you are hearing*

Hidden, unconscious messages expressed by the body can show us what emotional issues need attention. This most often applies to minor, recurrent complaints that have no obvious physical basis (or had a physical basis, but resist healing). You can find more detailed lists of ailments and emotional or spiritual causes in books such as Louise Hay's landmark *Heal Your Body* (see page 142 for more); the examples on the opposite page are to lead you toward an understanding of how intuitive knowing can manifest physically if its messages are suppressed or ignored.

Pay attention to what you feel in your body right now. Are there aches and twinges; or are you feeling focused, well, and energetic? You might experience a combination of these. If your body could speak, what would it tell you? Can you connect with the underlying thought of any dis-ease, and give it attention?

Working
WITH Guides AND
FINDING YOUR MUSE

Creativity can be understood as a
spiritual practice, a way to connect
not only with our intuition but also with
other realms.

For you, this may be the universe, the Source, All-That-Is, or God, or a legion of angels, guides, and muses. Creativity can be seen as an act of affirming the spiritual: stained-glass windows, illuminated letters, and mandalas are artifacts of devotion. Chinese calligraphy harnesses the flow of chi energy, the spirit of the universe. We honor those who have died through memorial tapestries, tattoos, museums, and monuments. Art is a way of making a connection with those who have inspired our lives, and with a beneficent, higher power.

As you develop your intuition you may become more open to sensing the presence of guides in your life. They may be someone you knew in this life who has passed on, a guide from another lifetime, or angels you sense around you. You might not see these guides with your physical eye in daily life, but you may intuit their presence.

Don't worry that you're imagining a sense of guidance. Our imagination—our ability to create through visualization—actually helps us link with the spiritual realms.

Here's an example. Imagine a scene—a waterfall, or fields—walk through it, and sit in a garden. Because the mind can't differentiate between real and imagined emotions, we begin to enter into this imaginary world in a real, emotional way. But then something else happens when we are not told what to expect. We may "see" a guide or angel during the visualization, or hear a name or message. This is because we are connecting with other realms and a consciousness outside our personal consciousness. The realm of guides and angels can be seen also as a metaphor for collective consciousness (see page 120): the idea that all the knowledge of humanity (past, present, and future) is available to us.

THE CREATIVE MUSES
Goddesses

Aoiode	Memory
Erato	Love poetry
Clio	History
Calliope	Epic poetry
Urania	Astronomy
Polyhymnia	Sacred poetry and hymns
Terpsichore	Dance
Thaleia	Comedy

Angels

Barachiel	Intuition
Vehuel	Creativity
Gabriel	Writing
Zadkiel	Performing
Metatron	Spirituality
Raziel	Mysteries
Ambriel	Solving problems
Eth	Being on time

Exercise: Calling in your muse

The concept of the creative guide has been around for eons. In ancient Greece, these guides were called Muses, which personified arts and sciences. For this exercise, choose your muse from the list on page 115 or mentally call upon someone you have known and admired.

1. Sit comfortably in a peaceful place where you will not be disturbed. Place the soles of both feet on the floor.

2. Close your eyes and take a deep breath. Visualize roots growing down from the soles of your feet into the earth, so that you are securely planted.

3. Imagine that you are stepping into a clear white bubble, which protects you spiritually.

4. As you breathe, visualize your breath as a stream of light, flowing through your roots, into your feet, up through your legs, and then through the center of your body right up to the crown of your head. Keep your focus on the breath and the stream of light, which now fills your body. Begin to tune in to the vibration of this pure, white light. You may feel lighter and more relaxed. If at any time you feel too floaty, return your attention to your roots to feel grounded once more.

5. Now say an invocation: ask aloud or in your mind to connect with your muse or angel. You might say, "Aoiode, please help me remember ...," or, "Angel Gabriel, please inspire me today as I write."

6. Feel your muse or angel standing behind you. Tune into your senses—you might feel a slight tingle on your skin, or sense a color or a faint scent. Stay with this until it begins to feel familiar.

7. When you are ready, thank your muse or angel, and visualize them fading behind you. Bring the white light down from the crown of your head, and back through your body to your feet. Step out of the bubble and bring your attention back to the room. Open your eyes.

More Ways
TO BE
More intuitive

Working with affirmation and oracle cards

Affirmation cards help you connect with your intuition by offering a range of unconscious triggers in the form of words and images. Psychics often use cards to give readings because they help them link with the energy of the sitter and the unconscious and higher realms, and bring relevant messages through. The cards act as a springboard for what is unseen.

Affirmation and oracle cards can generate a sense of purpose, offering insight and inspiration, and they are also an accessible way to tune in to the intuition frequency. You can choose one of the many affirmation or oracle decks available (see page 142), make your own using words or phrases (see the instructions for Oblique Strategies cards, page 98), or experiment by writing out a set of 11 cards or pieces of paper with one number on each. The meanings can be as follows, or you can invent your own:

1 New beginnings, ideas
2 Love, friendship
3 Creativity, productivity
4 Stability, planning
5 Negotiation, challenges
6 Harmony, peace, balance
7 Endurance, work
8 Travel, change
9 Self-expression, determination
10 Finding completion
11 Trusting your intuition

As another alternative, take blank cards or pieces of paper and some colored writing paper, crayons, or paints, and color them as you choose. The colors can have any meaning you like, or you can follow those listed here, which are traditionally associated with the body's chakras, or energy centers:

Red: Security, foundation
Orange: Creativity
Yellow: Energy, wisdom
Green: Healing
Pink: Love, compassion for the self and others
Blue: Truth, communication
Purple: Intuition, messages from the subconscious
White: Spiritual guidance or spiritual attitude

To go a step farther, create your own cards, using the colors above as a starting point for each card and adding more colors and cards as you like. Draw or paint the images that come to you, or collect magazines and cut out pictures to make a collage for each card. Some oracle decks contain 52 cards (the number of weeks in the year), while angel oracle decks often contain 44 cards, as this is deemed to be the number of the angels. You might begin with a small number of cards (11 for the 11 numbers above, or seven color cards), then gradually create more over a period of time as inspiration strikes.

TIP: INTUITION'S MAGIC WORDS

Many people who use their intuition for a living, such as psychics and mediums, avoid the use of the word "think" when they are working, and instead begin a sentence with "I feel …" or "I see …." They believe that this language sets an intention, telling the brain that the medium will connect with their right hemisphere, the home of intuition and emotions. Saying "I feel" or "I see" gives the right brain permission to talk.

Try it now: say "I feel" or "I see," and sense where your attention goes in your body. Now say "I think." It feels different, doesn't it? Julia, a medium, describes this as follows: "It's as if 'I feel' is coming from my heart area, while 'I think' goes straight to my head."

Try saying "I feel" or "I see" for a morning, and see if your communication feels more intuitive and authentic.

Exercise: Quick tune-in

Shuffle your cards or pieces of paper.
Ask a question, such as:

"What do I need to know today?"
"What will inspire me today?"
"What should I avoid today?"

Take one card from the top of the deck and turn it face up.
What do you see? Interpret it according to the words or image
on the card, the number, or color. Use your feelings to intuit the
meaning that is right for you.

Exercise: Past, present, future

Shuffle your cards or pieces of paper. Take three from the top of
the pile, and lay them out in a row. Now turn them over and
interpret each according to the words or image on the card, the
number, or color, as follows:

1 Past   2 Present   3 Future

Again, tune into your feelings to interpret each card, then begin
to construct a story (your left brain jumps in here, to make the
connections between the cards).

What's your story?

INTUITION AND ORIGINALITY:
The Collective Unconscious

You may have tried some of the exercises in this book, and I hope you will have felt inspired to **nurture your creativity**. But what if you have that lightbulb moment, that idea, and set out to develop it … but find that someone else has had exactly the same idea before you, or even at the same time?

Rather than seeing this synchronicity as negative, you could see it as a sign that you are tapping into what the twentieth-century psychiatrist Carl Jung termed "the collective unconscious." This is the concept of a realm of consciousness, potentially shared by all humanity, which operates outside our individual, personal unconscious. The collective unconscious can be imagined as being like a psychic internet, which contains our shared knowledge and experiences organized as a series of archetypes. While this begs huge questions about the nature of originality—nothing we create can be truly original, if it has been available to us for all time—the concept of the collective unconscious presents us with the idea of infinite possibility in creative terms. There are potentially no boundaries to what we might write about, or imagine, or create. And yes, our contemporaries and ancestors may have done all this before. But what makes creativity worthwhile to us is our interpretation: how we choose to express our ideas. The expression is unique to us, because we are uniquely ourselves, while sharing a universal human connection.

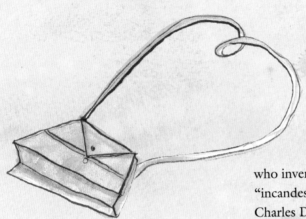

Alice hit on what she termed "a completely new" concept for a purse (handbag) design. "But about two weeks after I came up with the idea and sketched out templates, I saw something on the internet almost identical to what I'd visualized. So there's no point doing it now, is there?" Alice's take on her first venture in coming up with a creative idea tallies with misconceptions of creativity and creative genius: that creativity means doing something that no one else has done before. In fact, that is just one aspect of creativity, which is rare (see page 7); and even then, the inventor will have been influenced, subtly or directly, by his contemporaries and by past inventors. We stand on the shoulders of those who have gone before us. Could Thomas Edison have invented the lightbulb without those who invented an inferior version of the "incandescent lamp" before him? Could Charles Dickens have written *The Pickwick Papers* in 1836 without Henry Fielding's *Tom Jones* (1749), one of the first works of prose to be identified as a novel?

Creativity is a continuum, an ever-evolving process. Our personal and collective unconscious is our resource, and our mentors our inspiration. As Salvador Dalí said, "Those who do not want to imitate anything, produce nothing."

CHAPTER SEVEN

TWENTY WAYS

TO BE CREATIVE EVERY DAY

These easy techniques are designed to spark your ingenuity and trust your creative abilities. Flick through the pages each day and choose a tip at random, or take 20 days and try out a new tip each day.

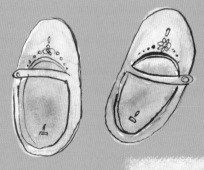

1 Set a Daily intention

Setting an intention is like **making a wish** or saying a prayer. Each morning you can set an intention for **the day ahead,** asking that your day turns out a certain way.

Making a wish is a form of manifesting, aligning your positive energy with universal energy to "co-create." By doing it, you acknowledge a divine source or higher power that can help your goal materialize.

You can speak your intention or write it down. Say, simply, what you would like to happen today (avoid saying what you don't want, as this gives energy to a negative statement). Your decision that your day should be a good, creative experience is powerful enough on its own—you don't need to be desperate, or have a grand goal in mind (in fact, desperation can block manifesting as, like negative statements, it brings negative emotion into the manifesting ritual).

Now feel your wish as if it has been granted. Generate a sense of joy, relief, relaxation—however you want to feel—and imagine it strongly. Add the timescale for your wish to be delivered (you can do a new wish every day, or set a longer timescale if you like), then consciously let go of the wish, with complete trust that you will get what you need. Place your manifesting "order" only once.

Go ahead with the rest of your day, but play close attention to your senses, along with conversations and communications (emails, phone calls, and texts), to make sure that you notice your gift arriving.

2 THE FiVE-MiNUTE Countdown

Here's a fast way to **get creative every day** in just

five minutes. First, set a deadline…

- The time you usually leave home in the morning (for work, school run, gym)
    —A time you need to leave to get to an appointment (doctor, optician, interview, meeting).
    —A time in the evening you need to leave to arrive at an event (a concert, meeting a friend, a class).

- Five minutes before you have to leave, take your Creativity Journal (see page 6) and write or draw in it for five minutes only. If you're writing, don't let the pen leave the paper. You can also write in the notes program on your phone, or type on your laptop. You might play the piano, start a poem, or sketch a mind map (see page 88). Don't stop until it's time to go, but do leave on time; you have just five minutes.

You might:

- Start with this sentence: 'Today there's rain/sun/gray skies; the last time I felt like this was …' Now continue.
    —Write down something you'd love to do and why.
    —Keep writing beyond the lists for the full five minutes, and you may well see an idea emerging at the end of the allocated time. Because you have just five minutes, you're not weighed down with self-expectation to produce a brilliant design or write a novel—and you just might spark off an idea that will lead to a project.

3 **Write** A SIX-WORD **Story**

Ernest Hemingway's famous six-word story, which he apparently wrote for a bet, reads: **"For sale: Baby shoes, never worn."** A lesser example is my friend Samantha's attempt: "Met, fed, bed, slept, left. End?"

You might try writing your six-word story in five minutes (see The Five-minute Countdown on page 125), using your own words or the words and phrases list on page 140 for inspiration. Or, set yourself a task to write a six-word story each day for one week.

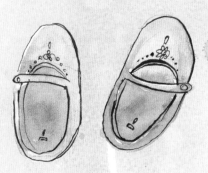

4 Make a Sound Diary

Download a recording app onto your phone or use Voice Memo. Go to a shopping mall, out for a stroll, or to an arts or sporting event, use public transport, or record snippets of conversation or activities in your home. You might **record your feet crunching through snow**, two people talking about a movie they watched, **or someone asking for directions**.

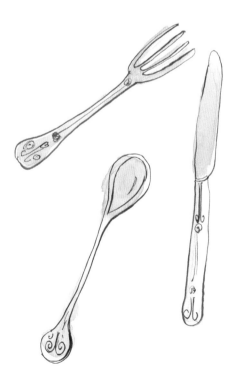

Play back your sound diary a day or two later. See how you naturally connect some of the sounds. Maybe words begin to sound rhythmic, or the sound of pots and flatware (cutlery) chiming in your kitchen begins to take on the form of a conversation. You might use this as your starting point for a piece of sound art, a story, or a poem.

127

5 Try A Binaural Beat

Creativity can be **enhanced** by sound, according to the developers of binaural beats. Binaural beats are sounds played at different frequencies to induce particular states of consciousness: **creativity,** meditation, better memory, pain management, relaxation, lucid dreaming, and deep sleep. A **binaural soundtrack** is best experienced through headphones, as sound of slightly different frequencies goes to each ear, to be processed by the brain as a beating sound. The brain becomes **"entrained"** to this pulse, matching its frequency.

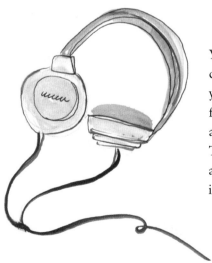

You can download a binaural app and choose an audio file according to how you'd like to feel, from an "espresso shot" for vitality through a creativity boost— a fascinating way to get into the zone. Try listening to a track before you begin a project and/or during work, and see if it helps your ideas flow.

6 Create
A NEW EMAIL
Sign-off

For your personal email accounts, add **something about you** after your usual signature.

At the start of the week, you might say: "This week, I'm thinking about beginning …" Or "I'm sending my support to the people of [country]," or "I'm proud to say that …" **Personal disclosure** means a lot to others. They see your values and attitudes and get to know you, which is vital if you're (digitally) marketing yourself and your projects; others need to know that you are open, curious, and authentic. You can also create a new email sign-off to help set your **positive intention** for the day or week (see page 124).

7 Make
SOMETHING
YOU'LL NEED FOR
YOUR Project

By making something that you will use for your project, you help **prepare yourself** for creative work without the pressure to begin the project itself:

- A journal decorated with your favorite motifs
- A quill pen from a feather
- A bag for your craft materials

If you're making music or if you're a meditation teacher, design your CD cover. Work around your project to keep the energy flowing.

8 Change YOUR Environment

You don't need to be at a desk or in a studio to be creative or work through a problem. In fact, going somewhere that feels impersonal to you is many **an artist's panacea.**

If you usually sit at a desk, go to a coffee shop (J. K. Rowling began writing the *Harry Potter* series in the back room of the Elephant House coffee shop in Edinburgh). If you're traveling, don't dismiss your hotel room as a creative space—there's an advantage to having no homely distractions. Maya Angelou chose to write her books in hotel rooms she rented by the month, although she had a house in the same town. She didn't sleep in the hotel, but went there in the mornings purely to write. She said: "I insist that all things are taken off the walls … I go into the room and I feel as if all my beliefs are suspended. Nothing holds me to anything."

10 Write it down Now

Keep a **pocket-sized notebook** with you wherever you go, or use your phone's voice recorder. **When you get an idea**, write it down or speak it.

We might vow to remember ideas, but in reality, we don't; there's always another distraction or conversation that diverts us almost instantly. Later, when you have time to work on your creative projects, play back or reread your collected notes and recordings. This is valuable material that will spark your imagination, and it's much better than facing a blank page.

9 Tweet a Curiosity

On your first trip out of the home this morning, **look around you.**

What appears different from yesterday? A mailbox hanging open, a huge cloud, a postal worker rushing to your neighbor's door with a parcel, flowers flattened by a rainstorm, one stiletto abandoned atop a trashcan? Take a photo. Does the photo tell a story? Tweet your photo in the spirit of curiosity: there's a wealth of difference between "Here's the lasagna I ate last night" and "Wonder what happened to that stiletto-wearer …"

11 Step INTO YOUR Alter Ego

Your alter ego is the most **compelling** version of yourself that you can imagine. Many movie and story plots depend on the tension between double identities—Clark Kent and Superman, Don Diego de la Vega and Zorro—or the secret heroism of "everyday" people: Eva, a grandmother in William Boyd's award-winning novel *Restless* (2006), had **a secret past** as a World War II spy, and **feared exposure** and **reprisals**. Authors themselves may opt for a different pen name when writing in a new genre, to liberate them from the pressure to succeed; for example, J. K. Rowling wrote her first crime novel, *The Cuckoo's Calling*, as Robert Galbraith.

Your alter ego may be villainous, glamorous, geeky, athletic, pedantic, or brave. How would this version of you respond to the email you've just read, the problem you're about to tackle, an event you're organizing? Your alter ego may just offer you an ingenious approach or idea.

You might choose a number of personas to suit your situation—call upon your incredible geek to hypothesize, or invoke the glamour goddess when you need confidence to go to a social gathering alone. Visualize your alter ego on your shoulder, taking charge.

12 Find THE Beauty:

RECYCLE "ORDINARY"

Artists excel in making **extraordinary** artworks from ordinary objects—from **cigarette sculptures** through mosaics made from M&Ms.

Arranging such mundane items en masse can give them new significance. Start a collection: every day, collect little pieces of the ordinary to make extraordinary: receipts from a store; public transport or dry-cleaning tickets; ring pulls from soda cans. Create a new context. You might begin with opposites, such as:

- Train or bus tickets: road/air transport theme (papier mâché birds …).
- Dry-cleaning receipts: water themes (boats, swimming, fish …).
- Junk mail: personal/impersonal themes (a collage of your family's names …).
- Plastic knives, forks, and spoons: fast food or fine-dining theme (a chandelier mobile from plastic teaspoons …).
- Try creating a physical sculpture or a video of you making your art, or arrange it on a flat surface and take a photograph.

13 Destroy!

The act of destruction in art is often seen as an act of **liberation**. In letting go of material possessions, we release our attachment to them—and create **a whole new perspective.**

British artist Michael Landy's performance piece Break Down (2001) consisted of a conveyor belt, a shredder, ten workers, and all his possessions—including his artworks.

Landy catalogued everything—7,227 items in all—then hired an empty store on Oxford Street, London's principal shopping street, and with his workers destroyed everything he owned, including his clothes and food, over two weeks. He received no payment for the work, and when it was over, he had nothing apart from the clothes he was wearing and his car. The work has been seen as a statement about consumption and consumerism.

Landy explains, "I had my own place to live, I had some furniture, I had some money in my bank account, then I stopped and thought about how I'm going to screw all this up … and what does this all mean, now that I can buy suits for £1,000? … and then it just came to me that I wanted to destroy all my personal belongings." Rather than feeling loss and regret, Landy experienced his installation, which attracted around 45,000 visitors, as "a really joyous occasion."

What could you make that is temporary, and what could you destroy or abandon?'

14 Design
YOUR DESK FOR
Creativity

Beginning each day with a small practical task **helps you prepare** for the mental tasks ahead.

Prepare the space first: clean the desktop and clear clutter. In feng shui, the art of placing objects to enhance positive energy (or chi), the desk can be divided into the nine sectors of the Ba Gua, an ancient map that links compass sectors with life areas. The creativity area is traditionally located center right on your desk. You can place your Creativity Journal (see page 6) here, along with any research notes, materials, collections, and notebooks, and keep it free from objects associated with problems (complaints, clutter, bills). This area is also linked with the element of metal, so metal items (paperweights or silver picture frames, for example) are believed to raise the chi energy here, giving your creative projects a boost.

15 Be an Active Listener

Today, be an "active" listener, ready to **engage fully** with everyone you encounter. Often, we don't listen enough: we begin a conversation with an agenda, hear the other person speaking, and, rather than **being open** to what they have to say, rehearse what we're going to say when they've finished.

TRY THIS: *Vow not to interrupt anyone today. You might be brimming with an idea you can't wait to blurt out, or you might think you know better than them, or you might be pushed for time and want to speed up the conversation. Resist. Slow down, and listen. They have something to share with you: receive it as a gift.*

When we listen actively, we step into a powerful place—the present moment, in which anything is possible. We're able to read the nuances in their language, really understand what they are trying to communicate, and respond appropriately. I'm sure you've met active listeners before—those people who make you feel you're the most important person to them, even for the one minute you share. They nod, gesture, and give you space to complete your sentences. They may repeat part of your conversation to ensure they've fully understood you. You feel they appreciate everything you have said, and that it's important. You feel good afterward.

16 Taking
iT ON

Tackling the most challenging situations at the beginning of the day **frees you up creatively.** Here's why...

If you put off that difficult phone call, meeting, or budget, guilt gathers (I know I should deal with this now, but I'd rather have a coffee/do the easy stuff first ...). This feeling sits between you and creativity, like a boulder in the road that you'd rather drive around than shift. Take on what you're resisting straight away. Blow up the boulder, and you're metaphorically free to drive up the creative highway for the rest of the day. Now you can focus on the parts of your job, or tasks at home, that you enjoy. And the more you enjoy what you do, the more creative you become. (For more on happiness, see Chapter 1.)

17 Reward
YOURSELF

Reward yourself without the excuse of a special occasion.

Have fun: try yoga karaoke (singing loudly to your favorite anthems as you do the Downward Dog), go to a movie on your own, take a two-hour bath. Invent ridiculous reasons to celebrate: bake a banana cake because it's Tuesday and it's raining. Hold a party in honor of a shelf you've managed to put up single-handed. Appreciate everything you do now; don't wait for someone to give you an Oscar.

If you struggle to appreciate yourself, get into an "attitude of gratitude." Write down everything you're grateful for, no matter how small (food, warmth, conversation, an easy drive, a smile). The common denominator for all these good things is you. Try this for one week, and see how your self-image shifts.

137

18 Be your Biggest Fan:
SELF-COMPASSION

Self-compassion isn't selfish. As self-compassion researcher Dr. Kristin Neff says, "the biggest reason people aren't more **self-compassionate** is that they are afraid they'll become more self-indulgent. They believe that self-criticism is what keeps them in line."

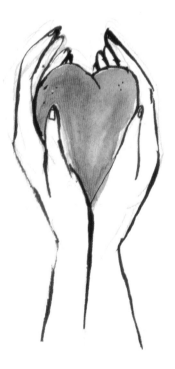

We're programmed to be "good" and put others first, but genuine kindness begins with self-compassion. When we understand our own needs and do our best to meet them, we can be compassionate to others appropriately, and without resentment. Be your own best friend. For today, do not criticize yourself. Accept all your feelings and treat them equally. As the thirteenth-century Persian poet and mystic Rumi said, "This being human is a guest house": we should invite in each morning's arrivals—our emotions—with joy.

19 **Relax** FOR CREATIVITY **Every Day**

A relaxed state of mind supports creativity. When we're relaxed, our thoughts are **positive**, we feel **happier**, and ideas flow. Choose one or more activity each day for yourself, just for relaxation:

- Listening to or playing music
- Movement: yoga, stretching, dancing
- Baking
- Rearranging a display
- Gardening
- Walking
- Tidying

20 **Repeat** YOUR RiTUALS

Decide how you want to prepare to get into **the creative zone.**

Rearrange your desk (see page 135), doodle, drink coffee, light a candle, pull an affirmation card, do a yoga stretch, listen to music, take a short, brisk walk, write a list … then make sure you repeat this ritual every time you begin, so your brain comes to recognize it as a sign that creative work will follow. Rituals can help reduce resistance to creative work, as they set up a rhythm that helps get you into the flow. You don't need to be a genius to be creative. You just need to be consistent in giving yourself time to create.

139

WORDS AND PHRASES

Your intuition is telling you

Less is more

Slow it down

Cross words

It doesn't always rain

Take time out

Peace

Too clever?

Music helps

Be still

Use a picture instead

See it in black and white

What's missing?

Look to the stars

Keep trying

Still waters

It's in the detail

Once upon a time …

Walk

Amazing grace

You know best

What if this is the last time?

My ideas are infinite

See the beauty

Finding answers

Stone circle

Be the teacher

Indulge

Blue

CHAPTER NOTES

CHAPTER 1
Creativity as the key to happiness
Jaak Panksepp's research: "Science of the Brain as a Gateway to Understanding Play: An Interview with Jaak Panksepp," *American Journal of Play*, vol. 2, no. 3 (Winter 2010), pp. 245–77

Creativity is easier when you feel positive
Research on mood and creativity: Mark A. Davis, "Understanding the Relationship Between Mood and Creativity: A Meta-analysis," *Organizational Behavior and Human Decision Processes*, vol. 108, no. 1 (2009), pp. 25–38

Matthijs Carsten K. W. and Bernard A. "A Meta-analysis of 25 Years of Mood-creativity Research: Hedonic Tone, Activation, or Regulatory Focus?," *Psychological Bulletin*, vol. 134, no. 6 (November 2008), pp. 779–806

Laughter as a creative tool
Lee S. Berk et al., "Neuroendocrine and Stress Hormone Changes During Mirthful Laughter," *American Journal of the Medical Sciences*, vol. 298, no. 6 (December 1989), pp. 390–96

Avner Ziv, "Facilitating Effects of Humor on Creativity," *Journal of Educational Psychology*, vol. 68, no. 3 (June 1976), pp. 318–22

Roger von Oech, *Expect the Unexpected or You Won't Find It: A Creativity Tool Based on the Ancient Wisdom of Heraclitus* (Berrett-Koehler, 2002)

Joe Hoare, Laughter Yoga: for blog and workshops, talks and book, *Awakening the Laughing Buddha Within*, go to www.joehoare.co.uk

The rebel doodle
Gwyneth Leech's coffee cups: www.gwynethsfullbrew.com

Graphic recording: Image Think: www.imagethink.net

CHAPTER 2
Benjamin Franklin's daily routine
Tim Goessling, "I Lived a Day According to Ben Franklin's Schedule and it Changed my Life," The Good Men Project, December 6, 2013; http://goodmen project.com/featured-content/dtv-benjamin-franklin

Time and resistance
Steven Pressfield, *The War of Art: Break Through the Blocks and Win Your Inner Creative Battles* (Black Irish Entertainment, 2002), p.35

Mindful ways to make the most of your time
Mark Williams and Danny Penman, *Mindfulness: A Practical Guide to Finding Peace in a Frantic World* (Piatkus, 2011)

Boredom
Hilaire Belloc, "A Guide to Boring," in *Hilaire Belloc: Stories, Essays & Poems* (Adeline Press, 1957); available at http://socialforthepeople.com

Getting the benefit … later
University of Central Lancaster study: S. Mann and R. Cadman, "Does Being Bored Make us More Creative?," *Creativity Research Journal*, vol. 26, no. 2 (2014), pp. 165–73

How are you bored?
Thomas Götz et al., "An Experience Sampling Approach," *Motivation and Emotion*, vol. 38, no. 3 (June 2014), pp. 401–19

CHAPTER 3
Keep a diary
Anaïs Nin, *On Writing* (Gremor Press, 1947); available at www.brainpickings.org/index.php/2013/09/20/anais-nin-on-writing-1947

Making art from memories
Bev Speight: www.mrsnorth.com

The gifts of limitation
Phil Hansen: www.philinthecircle.com

The dyslexia connection
Talks by Professor Julie Logan (www.youtube.com/watch?v=ItuDcJzKzvI) and Larry Banks (www.youtube.com/watch?v=AU-t061RuDU) at the Conference on Dyslexia and Talent (2013), organized by Dyslexic Advantage (www.dyslexicadvantage.com)

Creativity as therapy
David Read Johnson, Mooli Labad, and Amber Gray, "Creative Therapies for Adults," in Edna B. Foa and T. M. Keane, eds., *Effective Treatments for PTSD: Practice Guidelines from the International Society for Traumatic Stress Studies* (Guilford Press, 2009), pp. 479–89

Alive Inside movie: www.aliveinside.us
Larry Winters: www.lawrencewinters.com and www.makingandunmaking.com

Sharon Salzberg, "There is Always Trauma in the Room," *Huffington Post*, September 18, 2009; www.huffingtonpost.com/sharon-salzberg/there-is-always-trauma-in_b_262287.html. See also www.sharonsalzberg.com

CHAPTER 4
How do we create?
Henri Poincaré is discussed in Margaret A. Boden, *The Creative Mind: Myths and Mechanisms* (Abacus, 1992), pp. 29–35

Moving into the right-brain zone
Richard Bergland, *The Fabric of Mind* (Viking, 1986)

Being committed
Jamal Edwards, *Self Belief: The Vision* (Virgin, 2013, six ebooks and paperback); see also www.sbtv.co.uk

Feeding the flow
Silvia Hartmann: www.silviahartmann.com/liveFor
David Mitchell's Twitter novel, The Right Sort, follow @david_mitchell

CHAPTER 5
Begin with the brainstorm
Helmut Lamm and Gisela Trommsdorff, "Group Versus Individual Performance on Tasks Requiring Ideational Proficiency (Brainstorming): A Review," *European Journal of Social Psychology*, vol. 3, no. 4 (Oct–Dec 1873), pp. 361–88

Mindmapping
Tony Buzan: www.tonybuzan.com/about/mind-mapping

Oblique strategies
Brian Eno and Peter Schmidt, *Oblique Strategies: Over One Hundred Worthwhile Dilemmas*:
www.enoshop.co.uk/product/oblique-strategies.html

CHAPTER 6
How familiarity breeds intuition
Talk by Patrick Schwerdtfeger:
http://tedxtalks.ted.com/video/Learned-Intuition-Patrick-Schwe

Working with affirmation and oracle cards
Check out www.aeclectic.net. This is a tarot website with an oracles section—you can see a selection of cards from each deck featured. Other notable decks to try are Denise Linn's *Gateway Oracle Cards* and Kyle Gray's *Angel Prayers Oracle Cards*

CHAPTER 7
Try a binaural beat
Brain Wave™—30 Advanced Binaural Brainwave Entrainment Programs (iPhone app)

Change your environment
Alice E. Vincent, "Famous Writers' Retreats: The Rooms Where Classics Were Created," *Huffington Post UK*, June 12, 2012;
www.huffingtonpost.co.uk/2012/06/11/famous-writers-retreats_n_1586807.html

Be your biggest fan: self-compassion
Dr Kristin Neff quoted in Tara Parker-Pope, "Go Easy on Yourself, a New Wave of Research Urges," *New York Times*, February 28, 2011;
http://well.blogs.nytimes.com/2011/02/28/go-easy-on-yourself-a-new-wave-of-research-urges; see also Neff's own website, www.self-compassion.org

BIBLIOGRAPHY

Sue Beer and **Emma Roberts**, *Step-by-step Tapping: EFT—The Amazing Self-Help Technique to Heal Mind and Body* (Gaia, 2013)

Margaret A. Boden, *The Creative Mind: Myths and Mechanisms* (Weidenfeld & Nicolson, 1990; repr. Routledge, 2003)

Brené Brown, *The Gifts of Imperfection* (Hazelden Information and Education Services, 2010)

Stuart Brown, *Play: How It Shapes the Brain, Opens the Imagination, and Invigorates the Soul* (Avery, 2010)

Julia Cameron, *The Artists' Way: A Course in Discovering and Recovering Your Creative Self* (Pan, 1995)

Dr. Patrizia Collard, *Journey into Mindfulness* (Gaia, 2013)

Mason Currey, *Daily Rituals: How Artists Work* (Knopf, 2013)

Liz Dean and **Jayne Wallace**, *44 Ways to Talk to Your Angels: Connect with the Angels' Love and Healing* (CICO Books, 2014)

Cassandra Eason, *Angel Magic: Angel Inspiration for Busy People* (Piatkus, 2010)

Louise Hay, *Heal Your Body: The Mental Causes for Physical Illness and the Metaphysical Way to Overcome Them* (4th edn., Hay House, 2004) *You Can Heal Your Life* (Hay House, 1984)

Roger von Oech, *Expect the Unexpected or You Won't Find It* (Berrett-Koehler, 2002) *A Whack on the Side of the Head* (Creative Think, 1983; repr. Business Plus Imports, 2008)

Nick Ortner, *The Tapping Solution: A Revolutionary System for Stress-Free Living* (Hay House, 2013)

Steven Pressfield, *The War of Art: Break Through the Blocks and Win Your Inner Creative Battles* (Black Irish Entertainment, 2012)

Becky Walsh, *You Do Know: Learning to Act on Intuition Instantly* (Hay House, 2013)

INDEX

A

affirmations 50, 51–2, 55, 117–18, 139
alter ego 132
art 60–1, 133, 134
attitude
  creative 84
  email sign-off 129
  of gratitude 137
  introvert-extrovert 93–4
  positive 15, 51–2, 124, 129, 138

B

binaural beat 128
boredom 44–7
brainstorming 71, 80, 81, 85–7, 91

C

cell phones 43, 61, 93, 125, 127, 131
challenges, approaches to 17, 90–6, 137
collaboration 80–1
collections, ordinary objects 133
collective unconscious 115, 120–1
commitment 76–7
communication, with others 80–1, 136
connecting experiences 7, 72, 80, 81, 95–6, 106
creative crunch 74
creative flow 69, 79
creativity
  blocks to 53–9, 87, 90, 111

collective unconscious 120–1
daily routine 123–39
forms of 7–8
and intuition 110–11
preparing for projects 129, 135
resistance to 36–40
restoring 6–7, 9
stages of 46, 70–3
as therapy 65–7
creativity journal
  doodling 22
  five-minute countdown 125
  mindfulness practice 43
  placement on desk 135
crowdfunding 80–1

D

daily routine 123–39
daydreaming 47
deadlines 37–40, 90, 125
desk, rearranging 135, 139
destruction 134
diaries 58–9, 127
doodling 20–3, 139
dyslexia 61

E

email, sign-off message 129
Emotional Freedom Techniques 99
emotions
  and imagination 115
  problems with 113
empowerment 49–67

energy
  managing 30, 31
  universal 124
environment, changing 130
evaluation stage 71, 73
exploratory creativity 8

F

fear, dealing with 55, 57–8
Feng Shui 135
fifty-five–five strategy 90–2
five-minute countdown 125
Franklin, Benjamin 35

G

graphic recording 23
guides, working with 114–16

H

happiness 12–15, 16, 52
health problems 112–13
home, expressing creativity 62–4

I J K

ideas
  brainstorming 85
  collective unconscious 120
  growing 69–81
  writing down 131
illness 112–13
Image Think 23
imagination 52, 114–15, 124, 131
inactivity 44, 47, 72–3
infographic exercise 34–5

inspiration flash 69, 70, 71, 73
intention, daily routine 124
introvert-extrovert switchover 93–4
intuition 105–21

L

Landy, Michael 134
lateral thinking 97–8
laughter 15, 16–19
left-handed people 73
limitations 60–1
listening 136

M

meditation 41, 42, 43, 75, 92
memories, using 58, 59, 95–6
mind
  boredom break 45, 46
  clearing 32, 99
  resisting creativity 37
  right brain 70, 73–5, 89, 107, 118
  unconscious incubation 46, 70
mind-mapping 88–9, 125
mindfulness practice 32, 41–3
motivation 37, 40, 46, 79
muse, finding 114–16
music
  awakening senses 109
  crowdfunding 81
  daily routine 139
  right brain role 74
  as therapy 66

N

negative feelings 56,
124

O

oblique strategies cards
9, 97–8
oracle cards 117–19
overthinking 43

P Q

partnerships 80, 81
perfectionism 56
personal vision 50–2
play, creative 11–27
    art of 14
    doodling 20–3
    laughter 15, 16–19
    pleasing yourself 24–7
pleasing yourself 24–7,
47, 76
Poincaré, Henri 46,
70–1
positive attitude 15,
51–2, 124, 129, 138
preparation stage 71,
72, 129, 135
problem-solving 71, 73,
83–103
procrastination 87, 91,
102–3, 137
projects, preparing for
129, 135

R

relaxation 139
resistance 36–40, 47
rewarding yourself 137
right brain 70, 73–5,
89, 107, 118

S

schedules, planning 38,
40, 47
self-acceptance 49, 50,
55
self-awareness 52, 79
self-compassion 138
self-esteem, improving
56, 137
self-expression 62–4, 66
senses, awakening
108–9
six-word story 126
sixth sense, creative
105–21
skills
    learning 38, 40
    limitations 60, 61
    uncovering 78–9
social media 80, 81
sound 127, 128
spiritual practice 114–
16, 134
stress 15, 16, 40, 43, 75

T

talents, uncovering
78–9
tapping 99–103
therapy 65–7, 99
Thought Field Therapy
99
thought walk exercise
92
time 29–47
    making 32–5, 56
    making the most of
    41–3
    managing 30–1,
    38–40
trigger vision 52
trust in yourself 110–11
tweet, curious photos
131

U

unconscious incubation
46, 70, 71, 72–3, 86
unconscious mind
106–8, 117

V

vision board 50, 51
visualization 52, 75,
109, 114–16, 132

W X Y Z

walking
    awakening senses 108
    daily routine 139
    mindfully 41–2, 43
    thought walk exercise
    92
writing
    brainstorming 87
    commitment 77
    deadlines 38–9
    dyslexia 61
    five-minute
    countdown 125
    new ideas 131
    pleasing yourself 26–7
    right brain role 74
    six-word story 126
    as therapy 67
    your life story 56–9

ACKNOWLEDGMENTS

Thanks to Professor Michael Young and
Chelsey Fox for their amazing support;
appreciation, too, goes to Kathy Hulme,
Jen Hykin, Kay Stopforth, Bev Speight,
Liz Cunningham, Claire Gillman,
Patrizia Collard, and all at CICO Books.